PRAISE F
YOUR STORY ADVANTAGE

"Bill didn't just write a book, he created a game plan to unlock the one thing no one else on this planet has: YOUR story. This is how you take your real, raw experiences and turn them into a powerhouse book that can skyrocket your impact, influence, and income."

—**Dean Graziosi**, serial entrepreneur and multiple *New York Times* bestselling author

"I've always believed in the power of stories to sell ideas, products, and services. Now you can unlock your own unique story advantage with Bill Blankschaen's *Your Story Advantage.* This book reveals how your personal message is a force multiplier for impact, influence, and income. Essential reading for authors, speakers, coaches, and entrepreneurs ready to amplify their unique voice!"

—**Kevin Harrington**, original "shark" on the hit TV show Shark Tank, creator of the infomercial, pioneer of the *As Seen on TV* brand, and cofounding board member of the Entrepreneur's Organization

"*Your Story Advantage* isn't just a book. It's a breakthrough. Bill doesn't just teach storytelling—he embodies it. With the heart of a friend and the precision of a master craftsman, he shows you how to uncover, own, and leverage the story you've lived to unlock the future you've been called to. Bill has spent his life helping leaders, creators, and entrepreneurs turn their lived experience into lasting impact. He sees what others miss, pulls gold from the places you've overlooked, and gives you the clarity, confidence, and language to lead with authenticity and power. He knows what it means to wrestle with your story, to carry both the pain and the purpose, and to rise with a message that changes others because it first changed you. *Your Story Advantage* will not only help you speak and lead more effectively—it will help you live more fully. Your story is not a setback. It's your superpower. And with Bill as your guide, it's finally time to use it."

—**Justin Roethlingshoefer,** cofounder of Own It Coaching, *USA Today* bestselling author

"It's rare to meet someone truly living their purpose—Bill is one of those people. When I felt stuck in 'The Knowledge Trap,' Bill and the StoryBuilders process helped me find clarity, confidence, and voice. With his insight and encouragement, I transformed my story into a bestselling book. If you're ready to tell the story only you can tell, Bill is the guide you've been looking for."

—**Mark Pentecost,** founder of IT WORKS! and bestselling author

"*Your Story Advantage* brilliantly equips speakers to craft a Meaningful Message that not only connects but compels. Bill Blankschaen shows how your unique story—when shared from the stage—becomes a force multiplier for your influence, impact, and income. A must-read for anyone who wants to stand out and serve from the platform."

—**Grant Baldwin,** founder and CEO of
The Speaker Lab

"If you've ever wondered whether your story matters, this book answers with a clear 'yes.' Bill helped me clarify my own story and gave me the courage I needed to share it with the world. I know firsthand how empowering his process is. His passion to heal people through authentic storytelling is something I deeply acknowledge and appreciate. In *Your Story Advantage,* Bill's authentic and encouraging voice gives you the tools and confidence to tell your story with purpose and impact. Every page is a reminder that your story is your greatest asset when you know how to share it well. It gives you a deep perspective into why each and every human story matters and how they hold the power to heal the world and make a lasting difference!"

—**Muniba Mazari,** Goodwill Ambassador UN Women
Pakistan, speaker, artist, humanitarian

"I had a story to tell and for years couldn't figure out how to get it from my head to paper. Bill and his team at Storybuilders took control of the process, and we worked together to get the story down on paper. It was nothing short of miraculous. I can't recommend this book enough for all storytellers that are like me—you feel like you have something to say, and organizing that something just keeps getting jumbled up. This book will help you organize your story into something that you can be proud of—and most importantly, in your own voice."

—Jeff Allen, inspirational clean corporate comedian, author of *Are We There Yet?*

"Bill is a true Happy Hustler. This book is a masterclass in storytelling with passion and purpose to make a positive impact. So if you want a proven path to increase your income and impact with your message, this is the book for you!"

—Cary Jack, CEO of The Happy Hustle, *USA Today* bestselling author

"Bill Blankschaen gets it—your story matters. With heart, clarity, and contagious passion, he helps you see the bigger picture and step into a life that's truly worth telling. If you're ready to turn ideas into real-world impact, Bill is the guide you want by your side, and the book *Your Story Advantage* is your manual."

—Rachel Miller, founder of Pagewheel

"Your story can give you an advantage. But only when you tell it well. Bill Blankschaen is a specialist in helping you do this. This book will guide you to clarity, understanding, and expressing your own unique story as never before."

—Jim Cathcart, author of *The Acorn Principle* and 26 other books

To all those who have a Meaningful Message to share. Your courage and commitment to contribute a verse to humanity's song—*to be a StoryBuilder*—will truly make the world a better place.

Thank you!

All proceeds from the sales of this book will support
adoption efforts to give children the opportunity to
identify their own story advantage
and live a story worth telling.

YOUR Story ADVANTAGE

A **Proven** Path to **Maximize**
Your **Impact**, **Influence**, & **Income**

BILL BLANKSCHAEN

Founder of *Story* BUILDERS

Story BUILDERS PRESS

CONTENTS

FOREWORD

There are moments in life when you stumble upon something that just clicks. A book, a conversation, a realization—it's as if a missing piece of your own puzzle suddenly appears, illuminating a path you always knew existed but couldn't quite see.

For me, connecting with Bill Blankschaen and the StoryBuilders team has been one of those moments. Our collaboration on *New York Times* best-selling books like *The Greatness Mindset* and *Make Money Easy*, has been more than just a professional partnership; it's been a journey of shared purpose, a deepening of understanding, and a powerful affirmation of what I truly believe: your story matters, you are enough, and you possess an inherent significance that the world desperately needs.

This isn't just another book you've picked up. What you hold in your hands right now is an invitation. An invitation to unlock the power of your own narrative, to embrace your unique voice, and to realize that the most profound transformation begins not by striving to be someone else, but by truly seeing and honoring the person you already are.

For years, through The School of Greatness, I've had the privilege of interviewing some of the most inspiring and successful individuals on the planet. I've delved into their triumphs, their setbacks, and their core philosophies. And what I've consistently found, woven into the fabric of every great success story, is a deep understanding of self, a commitment to healing, and a willingness to share their authentic journey. We often chase external markers of success—money, fame, accolades—believing that these will bring us fulfillment. But time and again, I've seen that true greatness, true impact, and true abundance stem from an internal foundation. It's about building a life that feels authentic, connected, and purpose-driven, and that process begins with your story.

Think about it. We are all walking, breathing collections of experiences, lessons, and aspirations. These are the threads that weave together the tapestry of who we are. Yet, how many of us truly embrace our story? How many of us understand its inherent value, not just for ourselves, but for others? Far too often, we dim our light, we censor our truths, we believe that our past defines our future in a limiting way. We allow the wounds of yesterday, the critiques of others, or the fear of judgment to keep us small. We convince ourselves that our narrative isn't compelling enough, that our voice isn't strong enough, or that our message isn't unique enough. This is the ultimate trap, and it's one I've seen many, including myself at times, fall into.

But here's the truth: Your story is your superpower. It is your unique differentiator. It is the bridge that connects you to others on a deeply human level. And as Bill says, only you can steward your story. When you share your story, not just the highlight reel, but the raw, authentic journey—the struggles, the breakthroughs, the moments of doubt and resilience—you create a resonance that intellectual arguments or perfectly crafted marketing messages simply cannot achieve. You invite connection. You build trust. You inspire action.

Your Story Advantage is a masterful guide to precisely that. Bill Blankschaen and his team have distilled years of wisdom and practical application into a roadmap that will help you excavate, refine, and amplify your own Meaningful Message. It's not about superficial strategies or quick fixes; it's about a profound journey of self-discovery that culminates in a powerful expression of who you are and what you stand for.

I've long championed the idea of holistic greatness—that true success isn't just about career achievements or financial wealth, but about cultivating a rich, full life across all dimensions: mind, body, spirit, and relationships. And this is where the healing aspect of our stories becomes so crucial. Many of us carry unresolved emotional baggage, past hurts, or limiting beliefs that prevent us from fully stepping into our power. These internal blockages impact our relationships, our creativity, our ability to connect, and ultimately, our capacity to share our true selves with the world.

When Bill talks about the Story Traps, he's tapping into these very internal hurdles. He's recognizing that the journey of sharing your story isn't just about crafting compelling narratives; it's about overcoming the psychological barriers that prevent us from valuing ourselves and our unique contributions. That's why this book isn't just a how-to guide; it's a profound invitation to engage in a process of self-healing and self-acceptance that will ripple out into every area of your life.

Consider the Message Maker phase Bill introduces, which focuses on your BrandStory. This isn't just about building a catchy tagline; it's about understanding "Who are you... really? At your core? What do you deeply value? What do you want to accomplish that really matters to you?" These are questions that demand deep introspection, questions that require you to confront not just your aspirations, but your authentic self. When you truly understand your core values and your deepest desires, you lay the foundation for a story that resonates because it's deeply rooted in who you are.

And then, Bill introduces the Message Multiplier—your book. As someone who has experienced the transformative power of writing books firsthand, I can tell you there is nothing quite like it. A book allows you to take your message, your wisdom, and your unique perspective and scale it in ways you never could imagine. Bill rightly calls it a force multiplier, extending your influence far beyond your immediate reach. My own books have allowed me to connect with millions of people, to share lessons I've learned, and to impact lives in ways that continue to humble and inspire me. That's the enduring legacy of a well-told story in book form.

But beyond the external impact, the act of writing a book itself is a healing journey. It forces you to clarify your thoughts, to synthesize your experiences, and to articulate your message with precision. It's a process of self-discovery, where you uncover hidden connections and deeper meanings within your own journey. This clarity, in turn, empowers you. It builds confidence. It allows you to speak and live with greater conviction.

And finally, the Message Monetizer—your Intellectual Property. This is where the rubber meets the road, where your impact and influence translate into tangible abundance. For many, the idea of monetizing their message can feel uncomfortable, even contradictory to the idea of serving others. But Bill brilliantly dismantles this by reframing money as a placeholder for value. If your message truly delivers value, if it helps people solve problems and transform their lives, then receiving compensation for that value is not only acceptable but necessary for sustainability and further impact. It allows you to continue to serve, to create, and to reach even more people.

In my own journey, learning to embrace the value I bring and to effectively monetize my message has been a crucial step in building *The School of Greatness* into what it is today. It's allowed me to invest in my team, to produce high-quality content, and to expand my reach globally. It's not about greed; it's about creating a sustainable model for impact. This book provides practical, actionable strategies for transforming your wisdom into valuable products and services, from memberships and workshops to coaching programs and digital masterclasses. It empowers you to create a thriving ecosystem around your message, ensuring its longevity and expanding its reach.

Ultimately, this book is about far more than just building a brand or making money. It's about living a life of purpose and fulfillment. It's about understanding that your unique experiences, your struggles, your triumphs, and your insights are not random occurrences but essential components of a powerful story meant to be shared. It's about recognizing that you are enough, exactly as you are, and that your voice holds immense significance.

Bill's insights and frameworks are designed to help you break free from the self-imposed limitations that hold so many back. He empowers you to heal the internal wounds that prevent you from sharing your truth, to clarify the chaos of your ideas, and to confidently step into the spotlight of your own story.

The world is hungry for authentic voices, for genuine connection, and for meaningful solutions. Your story, with all its complexities and nuances, is a gift that only you can give. It has the power to inspire, to uplift, to transform, and to heal. It can change how people think, which in turn changes how they act, and ultimately, changes the world.

So, as you turn these pages, open your mind and your heart. Be willing to do the work. Be willing to reflect deeply. Be willing to embrace the messiness of your own journey, knowing that within that messiness lies the raw material for your greatest impact. This book is a powerful catalyst for that transformation.

Get ready to unlock your story, step into your greatness, and truly change the world.

To your greatness,

—Lewis Howes
Host of *The School of Greatness* show and *New York Times* Bestselling Author of *The Greatness Mindset* and *Make Money Easy*

Start with Story

There was a time when my day job was leading a private school. I was doing a lot of good and helping a lot of people. I loved the hugs I got from smiling kindergartners each day and the joy that came from guiding young adults through such a critical season of life. But as each day passed, I had to admit to myself that I felt stuck. I wasn't doing what I knew deep down in my soul that I was truly called to do.

You see, for nearly my entire life, I had told myself I was a writer—but I wasn't writing. I thought of myself as a storyteller, but I wasn't telling stories. Oh sure, I occasionally told a few stories in classrooms, and I knew I had great ideas and messages that could help a lot of people, but I didn't have time to work on them. I also didn't know how to get those ideas and messages out into the world. But knew that if I didn't figure out how to do that, I would regret it forever.

So I made one of the hardest decisions of my life up to that point. I chose to step away from my safe, secure job to pursue my dream of becoming a writer and a storyteller. I had a family to provide for, but we went without an income for the next year. And I never worked harder in my life.

I knew I could crack the code on writing and publishing; I just had to do my homework first. I talked with every publisher I could find and learned all about how the book world works. I created numerous book ideas and proposals, and shopped them to publishers. Most importantly, I became a student of storytelling technique—the science and art of communicating messages well.

To be candid, there were plenty of months that year that my wife and I didn't know how we would make the mortgage payment or buy groceries. That Christmas, all we could afford to give our six children was their own case of soda and a box of their favorite cereal.

I remember one afternoon in particular when I was sitting in the backyard with my pen and paper, trying to write. I heard birds chirping in the trees and smelled the spring flowers blooming around me. I was surrounded by the sounds of life on the outside and wrestling with my darkest fears on the inside.

As I stared into the woods that day, I felt as if I were sitting in the middle of a road at the bottom of a steep hill. As I looked up, I could see an eighteen-wheeler tractor trailer loaded with steel, barrelling down that road right at me—with no brakes. There was nothing I could do about it. All I could do was what I was called to do—sit in the middle of that "road" and write. I had to trust that if I leaned into my story, good things would follow.

So I kept moving forward. Finally, I did get my first publishing deal and wrote my first book. In fact, it was the very book idea I was working on that day as I stared down that dream-crushing tractor trailer. It felt great, but more importantly, I learned that I was really good at writing books. I began helping other people bring their books to life. I started helping them elevate their own messages so they could make more money.

Now, I get to do every day what I know I am called to do. I get to write and help people tell their stories in a way that makes the world a better place. And to this day, our kids say that the "cereal-box Christmas" was one of the best ever.

You see, I believe your breakthrough begins when you start with your story. That's why I started StoryBuilders. Over the past ten years, StoryBuilders has helped people just like you take a meaningful message and bring it to life to benefit others in a way that multiplies impact, influence, and income. And it's those same proven storytelling techniques that I want to share with you—because the world needs to hear what you have to say.

ONLY YOU CAN SHARE YOUR STORY

What do I mean by *story*? I don't mean simply what has happened to you. The events of your life are certainly part of your story, but I mean far more than simply a record of your activities on this earth. In fact, I would put it like this: Your story is your Meaningful Message told in your unique style to serve a specific need.

> **Your story is your Meaningful Message told in your unique style to serve a specific need.**

Your Meaningful Message is the message that burns within you, the one you are passionate about sharing with the world. It's what moves you at the soul level. For example, my Meaningful Message is simple: Every story matters, and when we tell our stories well, we make the world a better place.

Whatever your Meaningful Message is, every time you tell it, you share it in your own style. Your uniqueness is where the magic happens. Other people could have a message similar to yours, but only you can share it in your own way, choosing specific words and particular patterns to express it. Think about it. What makes you unique? No one else has your experiences. No one else has gone through what you have gone through. No one else has experienced your highs and lows, your wins and losses. Those experiences have shaped your perspective on life, the universe, and everything in it. No one else has your distinct credentials, your mistakes, or your lessons learned. In short, no one else is *you*.

Wisdom literature throughout the ages has affirmed that there is nothing new under the sun. However, *you* are new. There has never been another you, so no one else could possibly have your take on your Meaningful Message because no one else has lived the life you have lived.

Yet simply having a Meaningful Message told in your unique style is not enough. To make the world a better place, your story must serve a specific need. For example, my Meaningful Message moves me to come alongside people who have a Meaningful Message of their own burning within them but struggle to tell it well and share it with the world. By helping those people—perhaps you—release that story to the world, I become a force multiplier, a story catalyst who empowers each of these people to multiply their impact, influence, and income. Thus, my story serves a specific need in the world as I live out my Meaningful Message in my own unique way.

You may be thinking that you don't really have an incredible, mind-blowing story or a tale of incredible events where you've overcome tabloid-worthy obstacles. Don't worry. In fact, whether you've lived what some consider a sensational tale has little to do with having a story worth telling. Some people will resonate more with an incredible sequence of life events, and others won't. But they will all connect with someone who sounds like they've had experiences similar to their own. It's all about connection. As you answer the call to clarify your Meaningful Message, you'll cultivate the courage to share it in your own unique way and begin to serve a specific need.

UNLEASH THE POWER OF YOUR STORY

This book isn't for everyone because not everyone wants to leverage their story to multiply their impact, influence, and income. And that's okay. That's not to say your story doesn't matter. It absolutely does. As I said earlier, every story matters (more on that in Chapter 8).

But in this book, I'm talking to these people:

- People who have already experienced a significant level of success sharing a message, building a business, leading a team, or rallying people around a cause.

  If that's you, you're probably making pretty good money by most standards. You have made an impact, and your influence has grown as you have grown. You've earned your success the hard way, so you're probably deeply invested in your business, personal brand, or organization.

  Most people would say you've done well. But truth be told, you feel like you could be—perhaps even *should* be—doing more. If only your story could reach more people. If only you could touch more lives. If only more people knew about what you do and how you can help them. But you're already busy doing good work, and you say you can't be an expert on everything needed to break through to next-level impact, influence, and income.

If this is you, here is what you need to do: *Start with story.*

- People who have a Meaningful Message to share with the world and want to build something sustainable around it. Perhaps you want to be a speaker, author, coach, consultant, entrepreneur, or leader in your chosen field, but you're not quite there yet.

  You're willing to work hard and learn and grow to get there, and you've even experienced some success so far. But you know you've still got a ways to go. So you're wondering, *How can I accelerate my progress? How can I bend my growth curve to move farther faster?*

  If that's you, the answer is the same: *Start with story.*

- People who have a side hustle they're trying to grow or a dream or message they want to share with the world. If that's you and you're not sure where to start, I'm so glad you found this book now before you get too far down the road.

  The same advice holds true for you: *Start with story.*

Here's why the same advice applies to all of you: Your story serves as a *force multiplier,* a catalyst for your success. It is a catalyst that, when told well, can accelerate everything you do. Think of it as a lever that when properly positioned can lift you higher than you imagine you could go.

It may help to think about it using The StoryMultiplier Formula™:

$$WHO \times S = I^3$$

WHO = Who you are. It includes:

- **Your behavioral** hardwiring and all the stuff you can't change about yourself, such as your strengths and struggles.

- **Your experiences.** Only you have lived your life in the way you have lived it. No one else in the history of the world has done that.

- **Your relationships.** Only you have been uniquely shaped by your connections with other people from an early age.

- **Your CQ, EQ, and IQ.** Your character quotient (CQ), emotional quotient (EQ), and intelligence quotient (IQ) all come together to shape who you are as you learn and grow.

S = Story and how well you tell it

All of who you are gets multiplied by how well you share your story with the world. The fact is that you could have powerful hardwiring, unbelievable experiences, incredible relationships, and amazing CQ, EQ, and IQ and still make little to

> All of who you are gets multiplied by how well you share your story with the world.

no impact on the world. It happens every day. Many people don't do anything intentional with their story. But those who do are in a position to experience multiplied impact, influence, and income.

I ^{3} = Impact, Influence, and Income

People who experience elevated levels of impact, influence, and income may not be better people. They probably don't have better stories. And they certainly don't have magical qualities that somehow give them a secret edge. But they have gotten intentional about telling their stories—and that makes all the difference.

WHAT'S STOPPING YOU?

Perhaps your instincts have told you that you have a unique message to share with the world. Maybe you've seen your story resonate with others and help them in significant ways. You may have already built a platform, a business, or a nonprofit around your story and experienced some success. But something seems to be holding you back from breaking through to the next level of influence. You may have unintentionally fallen into one of the following five most common Story Traps.

1. **The Confidence Trap: You diminish it.** We tend to deify others and diminish ourselves. Call it human nature, if you will, but it happens too often to be a coincidence. It's so easy to think that someone else has an amazing story to share with the world, but not you. After all, you've lived your story, so it feels normal to you. But here's the thing: the same is true for the people you deify. Their stories feel normal to them too. But that didn't stop them from putting their stories out there and experiencing breakthrough success as a result.

   > We tend to deify others and diminish ourselves.

2. **The Chaos Trap: You paralyze it.** There is a common problem that I call the Creativity Conundrum: *The more creative ideas you have, the harder it is to get any of them done.* For those who *do* see the value of their story, this trap often keeps them stuck. There are so many good messages they could share, so many interesting ways to tell them, and so many opportunities to pursue—so they chase all of them just a little bit and move none of them forward in a significant way.

3. **The Normalcy Trap: You undervalue it.** Normal feels not valuable. Because you have lived your story,

thought your thoughts, and been shaped by your message, you can easily miss the potential they have to multiply your impact, influence, and income. But the truth is that there are many people in the world who would be drawn to you if you told your story well. And those people simply may never be drawn to others whose stories you think are more amazing than yours. What feels not valuable to you is exactly what someone else needs.

4. **The Hidden Cost Trap: You waste it.** Don't get me wrong. You don't intend to waste your story. But unless you realize what it is costing you *not* to steward your story well, you're simply unaware of the high cost of doing nothing. If only you had a magic mirror to see the missed impact, influence, and income—but at least you have this book. That's a start. (You can try nailing it to the wall and talking to it, but for better results, I suggest you just keep reading.)

5. **The Knowledge Trap: You don't know what to do with it.** Ignorance is a valid excuse, but it is also the easiest trap to escape. In fact, all you have to do to escape it is to keep reading.

If any of these traps feel familiar to you, don't worry. Like I said, they're common. In spite of feeling the weight of these traps, you are sensing the call to tell your story well and share your message in a way that multiplies your impact, influence, and income.

For many of us, the call comes from somewhere deep within our souls. For me, the call has a divine urging to it that is fueled by my faith in God. For others, it feels more pragmatic—they know they can help more people and make more money while telling their story. For others, it's more about creating a legacy that continues to make an impact around the world for generations to come. For all of us, it feels like a responsibility to steward our stories well.

Here's a deeper truth that is both liberating and potentially unnerving: *Only you can steward your story.*

Only you can steward your story.

This truth hit me hard at that pivotal moment when I chose to step away from the school. I found it difficult to lean into my own story since doing that felt at odds with my identity at the time. Yes, I always saw myself as a writer and storyteller, but I also saw myself as a teacher and leader who helped others grow in their faith and knowledge. I was known in the community as *the guy* who leads *that* school. And it was a truly great school. We were doing terrific work, helping hundreds of students and families, partnering deeply with them to walk alongside them through the good and the bad. In short, I felt like I was doing God's work on a daily basis, which made it more difficult to consider leaving that role.

While it might seem like I just woke up one day and said it was time to leave, the decision to step away from that role was actually a two-year process. I had felt something shift inside my soul. I wrote the following quotation by William H. Murray on an index card and put it where I would see it every day:

> Until one is committed, there is hesitancy, the chance to draw back. Concerning all acts of initiative (and creation), there is one elementary truth, the ignorance of which kills countless ideas and splendid plans: that the moment one definitely commits oneself, then providence moves too.
>
> All sorts of things occur to help one that would never otherwise have occurred. A whole stream of events issues from the decision, raising in one's favor all manner of unforeseen incidents, meetings and material assistance, which no man could have dreamed would have come his way. I have learned a deep respect for one of Goethe's couplets:
>
> Whatever you can do or dream you can, begin it. Boldness has genius, power and magic in it. Begin it now.

That morning, I committed to stewarding my story better. I didn't know exactly what that meant, but I had chosen to take ownership of it and figure it out. For the next two years, I tried to do both: pursue my calling to write and tell stories at night, and run a school committed to excellence by day—and do it all without neglecting my wife and our six children.

Needless to say, it created some tension. After a year and half, I felt like I wasn't doing any of it well. I finally reached the place where the pain of staying put was greater than the fear of stepping out.

I reached out to a mentor and got his advice. I enlisted a life coach to help guide me. I went on a retreat to find my focus and try to figure out how to do it all. On that retreat, I finally came to this key realization: *I can't.* Either I needed to go all in with the school or all in with my calling. In that moment of decision as I sat in a quiet log cabin beside a lake, I embraced this powerful truth: Only I can steward my story. Someone else can run the school.

I immediately felt like a vise had released me. Even though it took several months to play this out, that day, I stepped out before I knew how it would turn out. I was determined to do what I felt called to do rather than what others wanted or needed me to do.

Like I said, it wasn't an easy road, and I am grateful for the many guides I met along the way. As a result of that choice, I had the privilege of founding and now leading StoryBuilders, a creative team that partners with people who want to elevate their messages to multiply their impact, influence, and income.

We've worked with incredible people you may have heard of—Lewis Howes, John C. Maxwell, Kevin Harrington from the hit TV show *Shark Tank*, and numerous others whose names you likely know. I became a multiple *New York Times* and *USA Today* bestselling writer who has worked on hundreds of books. Now our team is on its way to helping more than a thousand StoryPartners tell their stories well and share them with the world. At first glance, that number may not seem like much, until you realize that each of those people we serve has a vision to touch tens of thousands, millions, and even billions of lives.

That's great, Bill, you may be thinking right now. *I'm glad that worked for you. But how do I leverage my unique story to multiply my own impact, influence, and income?*

I'm glad you asked because I wrote this book for you.

YOUR STORY ECOSYSTEM™

In the pages to come, I'll share with you the proven process I've learned from studying those who have paved the way. I'll show you what I learned from my own journey and a decade of working closely with hundreds of influencers, entrepreneurs, business leaders, and voices of all sorts to help them elevate their messages.

It begins with this: Every story, including yours, has an ecosystem, the natural living space in which your story thrives and expands. When you intentionally cultivate it, you begin to break through your barriers and position yourself and your team to multiply your impact, influence, and income.

Here's how it works.

1. **The Message Maker: Your BrandStory.** Your story begins when you make your message clear. Most people skip this step and end up wondering why they feel like they're all over the place. Don't be that person. Don't lead that organization. Get clear on your story and prepare to grow. I'll show you how to do this in Chapter 3.

2. **The Message Multiplier: Your Book.** Nothing captures your message like a book. Nothing gives you an instant credential that opens so many doors for you. You literally become the person who wrote the book about [insert your message here]. If you lead an organization, a book can do more for your cause than you might realize. In Chapter 4, I'll teach you how to start multiplying your message through writing a book.

3. **The Message Monetizer: Your IP.** Intellectual property—that's what we call how you present and package your unique ideas to the world. What most people don't know is that your IP can become the key to making not just more money but a *lot* more money. In Chapter 6, I'll walk you through how to monetize your message.

Your *Story* EcoSystem®

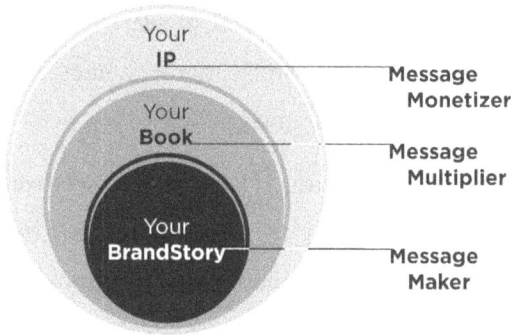

If you stick with me, I'll guide you through each of these steps and equip you to make significant progress on them right away. I'll take you behind the scenes and reveal the same proprietary process StoryBuilders uses all day, every day to build stories and create Meaningful Messages for people you've heard of and a lot of others you don't know about—yet.

The question for you is this: Will you choose to answer the call to steward your story well?

Only you can answer that question because only you can do it.

When I was stepping out from the school, I took a trip to Manhattan for an event led by marketing guru Seth Godin. That event was inspired by a blog post Seth had written that included these words:

Our cultural instinct is to wait to get picked. To seek out the permission and authority that comes from a publisher or talk show host or even a blogger saying, "I pick you." Once you reject that impulse and realize that no one is going to select you—that Prince Charming has chosen another house—then you can actually get to work.

If you're hoping that the HR people you sent your resume to are about to pick you, it's going to be a long wait. Once you understand that there are problems just waiting to be solved, once you realize that you have all the tools and all the permission you need, then opportunities to contribute abound.

No one is going to pick you. Pick yourself.[1]

After the event, I chatted with Seth. I was carrying a small notebook that was inspired by the creative energy of Walt Disney. Seth signed it with such passion that his pen ripped into the pages, leaving an indelible mark, not only on the notebook but also on my soul.

I want that same passion for you. I want you to feel the call to share your Meaningful Message with the world so powerfully that you rip through the pages to come.

Pick yourself—because the world needs to hear what you have to say.

YOUR ADVANTAGE ACTIVITIES

Over the course of this book, I will take you through the process of creating and sharing your story well so you can maximize your impact, influence, and income.

But before we start that process, take a moment to reflect on a couple of questions. If you have a journal or notebook, feel free to write your answers there. I simply want to help you start the process of stewarding your story.

1. What is the Meaningful Message at the core of your story? Have you distilled your calling or purpose into a single sentence or idea? Or is it still just a series of stories and anecdotes floating around in your mind?

2. Are you stuck in a Story Trap? If so, which one(s) tends to hold you back the most? Why do you think that is?

3. To what extent have you started sharing your Meaningful Message? How have people responded? What expressions or phrases have resonated most with people when you share them?

The key to this whole process is answering the call to share your story well because breakthrough begins when you choose to start with your story.

When you do, there's no limit to how far your story advantage can take you.

The Art and Science of Storytelling

I f I were to say, "It all started with a mouse," you'd probably know who I'm talking about. But *why* would you know that?

Walt Disney pioneered many innovations and inventions, but his greatest legacy is the generations touched by the stories he told—and how he told them.

Through his many failures and experimentations, Disney learned that the art of storytelling is at least as important as the story being told. Fresh off winning back-to-back Academy Awards in 1932 and 1933, he announced the creation of his studio's first feature-length film: *Snow White and the Seven Dwarves.* By then, Snow White's tale had been told many times, from the Grimm Brothers to a stage play, a silent film, and more. Disney knew he needed more than new animation technology such as the multiplane camera to bring the story to life. He would need lovable characters to capture the audience's hearts, the theme of a dream in peril of never coming true, and then a happy ending—with touches of comic relief throughout. This approach came to be known as the Disney way of telling familiar stories from a fresh perspective.

The success of *Snow White* helped Disney grow Disney Brothers Cartoon Studio into the Walt Disney Company by taking familiar stories and characters and putting them into a reliable storytelling pattern infused with elements that invoke our strongest emotions. Not every Disney movie features a love story like the one in *Snow White*, but they all have the same basic elements and structure that essentially follow the classic Hero's Journey pattern that great storytellers have used for millennia.

Think about some of the Disney movies you've seen. *Pinocchio* was an Italian children's story from the 1880s that Disney updated with his proven storytelling elements and structure. *Beauty and the Beast* took a classic tale and infused new energy into it by using the same approach. The same is true of *The Little Mermaid*. Even *The Lion King*, inspired by Shakespeare's *Hamlet,* received the Disney treatment.

More recently, hits like *Frozen* and *Frozen 2* have taken Norse legends and repackaged them using Disney's simple but powerful structure (and adding a few songs you just can't get out of your head once you hear them). Likewise, *Moana,* inspired by Polynesian culture and myths of the demigod Māui, was run through the same proven storytelling process.

All of them follow that pattern. Good stories are like that; they all feel similar but also somehow different. They feel comfortable and yet fresh at the same time.

Maybe you've experienced that feeling when traveling abroad. I once visited Japan with my family and found that everything looked sort of familiar to me. Roads, traffic signs, housing, vehicles—all of them resembled what I was used to seeing, and yet all of it was unique to Japanese culture. The vehicles were more compact, the housing was more efficient, the signs were close enough to English to make sense of them, and the toilets—well, don't even get me started.

Good stories are like that; they all feel similar but also somehow different.

On the other hand, when I went to Vietnam, there was less familiarity, which made my stay there feel less comfortable. The tangled web of electrical lines hanging precariously between buildings, the millions of mopeds and motorcycles somehow managing to miss each other on the busy streets, the many people living on boats along the crowded waterways— they all caused me to feel displaced. Neither place was necessarily better or worse; I simply connected more with the Japanese setting than the Vietnamese setting. I felt both drawn in by the familiar and intrigued by the differences.

I think about this dynamic as The Connection Continuum:

Too Different = Disconnection

Too Similar = Duplication

Just Right = Drawn In

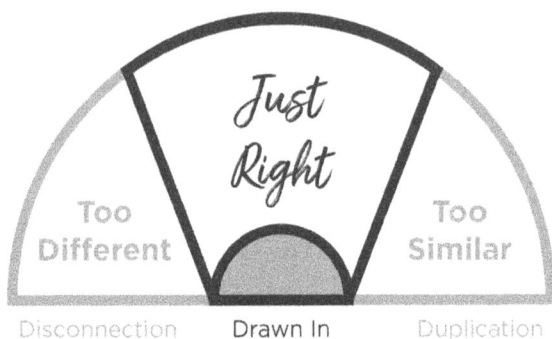

So it is with telling your story. If your message is told in a way that is simply too different from what people know, they will disconnect from it. On the other end of the continuum, if it sounds just like all the other stories they've ever heard, they can easily dismiss it as a duplicate. The trick is to find the balance between both, to get it "just right" so the people you want to reach are drawn in. And the best way to do that is to use a proven process.

The reality is that anyone can tell their story, and some can do it well; however, when you start with a proven structure, you're more likely to finish with a powerful message.

OVERCOMING THE FEAR

If you've ever been stuck staring at a blank page, unsure of what to do first or next, you're not alone. Even Disney had days when he couldn't quite pinpoint why a drawing didn't work or what was missing from the story. And I've certainly been there too. Remember that sunny day I told you about in Chapter 1? That was rough.

Everyone experiences this dreaded phenomenon. Some call it writer's block, the blinking cursor, or the blank page. Whatever you name it, I'm talking about the fear that you won't be able to tell your story well because you simply don't know where to start.

Maybe you're trying to write an email introducing a new policy to your employees, but you can't decide how to phrase it. Or maybe you have to draft a white paper on a new product you'll be rolling out to your clients, but the voice of your high school English teacher pops into your head, telling you that you're terrible at writing.

Whatever the cause of your paralysis, a proven can set you free. Once you have momentum, everything gets easier. Better still, when you know the plan you're following is based on classic storytelling techniques, your fear dissipates, and you begin to make progress faster.

I became a student of story at an early age. I was always an avid reader, even as a child. I would spin the cereal box at breakfast, reading every word five times, even the ingredients I couldn't pronounce. During my teen years, I soaked up books of all sorts. I even bicycled several miles to our local library on Saturdays so I could sit in a corner and read Shakespeare. (Yes, I was *that* nerd.) I loved stories and learned all I could from the masters.

My love of stories prompted me to start writing my own. I created a fictional detective character when I was eight years old and typed the manuscript (yes, using a typewriter and lots of Wite-Out) on hand-cut pages. I then gutted and papered over the cover of another children's book and put my pages inside. (I never finished the story after the second murder, so I never figured out who did it. But I don't think that early attempt at writing would have been a bestseller anyway.)

After getting degrees in English and history, studying the masters and their works, and then teaching them for decades, I discovered that there is a natural storytelling pattern we humans look for that draws us in and feels familiar—something Disney hit on too.

Some people have written thick books on detailed storytelling techniques, so if you want to dive deeper, there are plenty of resources out there to help you. But I want to give you a simpler process you can use when communicating anything, from a blog post to a book, from a memo to a masterclass, or from a social media reel to a really engaging website about you or your brand.

Instead of feeling like you must start with a blank page, you can leverage this proven process to tell your story well and get started.

Like many things, good storytelling requires both *art* and *science*. That blend shouldn't surprise us because we see it everywhere.

- **Architecture:** Frank Lloyd Wright pulled inspiration from the environments around his buildings and houses to create lasting structures that blended in and highlighted the natural beauty of those settings.

- **Music:** Every song is a blend of someone's artistic expression united with physics and math—frequency, pitch, and sound waves.

- **Cooking:** Great chefs know you have to balance flavors and textures to create a great dish. Great bakers know you have to balance creative flair with scientific precision to create a great cake.

- **Driving:** The best Formula 1 or NASCAR drivers all started by learning the mechanics or structure of driving techniques and what makes the car go faster. But what separates the good from the great is the art of maneuvering the car in and out of traffic at exceptionally high speeds.

- **Golfing:** Anyone who has ever tried to golf knows it takes the solid structure of a sound swing to have any chance of being decent. But the best players take it to the next level. Once they have gotten great at the structure, the game becomes about finesse in execution, both in mindset and artistry on the links.

I could go on, but examples are literally everywhere. Even a printed book unites the science of precise paper size and binding with the creativity of the interior and cover to produce a book worth reading. You don't have to consider yourself a scientist or an artist to recognize the need for both science and art to bring something truly masterful to life.

THE STORYTELLING STRUCTURE™

The StoryTelling Structure™ is drawn from classic storytelling techniques humanity has used for thousands of years. It is not intended to be exhaustive and works best when communicating about nonfiction topics. In other words, it is not meant to be a formula for writing the next great novel, although it could be helpful if that's what you want to do.

Understanding this simple but powerful structure positions you to tell your story and any story most effectively in order to connect with your intended audience.

The *Story* Telling Structure®

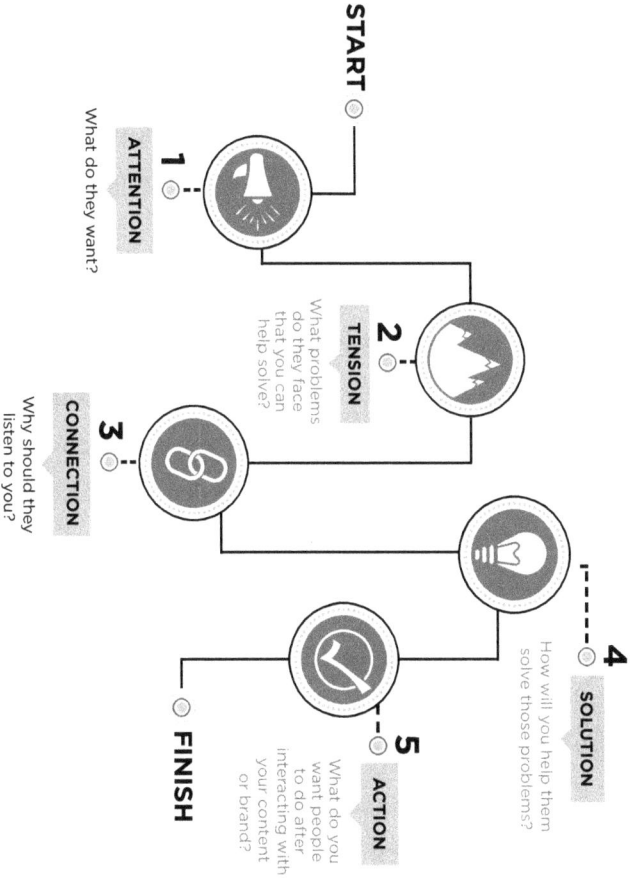

START

1 ATTENTION
What do they want?

2 TENSION
What problems do they face that you can help solve?

3 CONNECTION
Why should they listen to you?

4 SOLUTION
How will you help them solve those problems?

5 ACTION
What do you want people to do after interacting with your content or brand?

FINISH

Here's how it works:

1. Attention. If you want to tell a story that people will listen to, you must first get their attention. That seems simple enough, but how do you do that? Is it by using strobe lights and a stage production? Well, maybe. It depends on who you're trying to reach and, most importantly, what *they* want. In fairytale terms, think of this as the treasure they seek.

2. Tension. Don't run from problems. Embrace them. In fact, a problem your audience has is an opportunity for you to solve it. Once you have your audience's attention, reveal the problems that keep them from getting what they want. Think of it as the fiery dragon that has stolen the treasure they seek.

3. Connection. This is where *your* story enters the plot. People want to feel a connection with you, so this is where you can be vulnerable. Share why you know what that problem feels like. Did you struggle with it too? How did it feel? What did you do? What they really want to know is the success you had overcoming it. Then you can share your …

4. Solution. The Solution section is often the bulk of your message. It lays out the process your audience can follow to solve the tension you highlighted earlier. Think of this as giving them a magical sword they can use to kill the dragon. In fact, this Solution step is where a lot of magic happens for you since it often forms the basis of the Intellectual Property (IP) you can monetize (more on that later).

5. Action. Finally, with the dragon out of the picture, there is always a path for your audience to go to the next level. Think of this as what they need to do to seize the treasure for themselves.

The StoryTelling Structure™ varies depending on the medium being used—book, video, course, keynote, and more. It's also important to both follow it and hold it loosely.

When it comes to communicating well, think of The StoryTelling Structure™ as the science part of the equation. Once you get used to using it, the structure becomes more like a set of guidelines that free you to tell your story in fresh, creative, and artistic ways—science *and* art.

Let's try it out with an example of a blog post I wrote some years ago that uses The StoryTelling Structure™ method:

Yawn!

When I read Michael Hyatt's post on taking naps, I agreed. I knew from personal experience how beneficial a quick midday nap could be. But as I pondered how I might actually put it into practice, I hit a wall. Maybe you felt the same thing?

How could I keep moving forward with this idea in an educational role that requires me to be always alert and on call throughout the school day? The tension between what I wanted to do and what I *could do* quickly threatened to become crippling frustration.

I suspect I'm not alone in feeling overwhelmed at times by excellent advice, helpful strategies, and enlightening insight. To be candid, sometimes I feel like a deer in the personal-growth headlights. I'm often paralyzed by the possibilities. It's easy to see where I want to go. It's figuring out how to get over the walls between here and there that creates the tension.

We usually think of tension as always being a bad thing. It can be. But growth always requires *movement*. And movement creates tension between where we are and where we're going. It's when we hit a wall—or what seems to be a wall—that we can get the wind knocked out of our dreams.

Here are a few ways you can keep moving forward when you hit a wall in your personal growth:

- **Screen for Excuses.** Be honest with yourself. It's easy to slip in an excuse disguised as an immovable barrier. To be safe, assume all walls are excuses until proven otherwise. Like Neo of *Matrix* fame, sometimes your best answer will be that "there is no wall."

- **Question the Walls.** You could try talking to them, I suppose, but that could lead to other problems. Think about the barriers themselves. Are they walls that you've created yourself or allowed to be created in your silence? Are you missing the skill sets to get over the walls? Where can you get a reliable third-party perspective on the barriers you face? Don't rule this out: The walls may be telling you it's time to grow elsewhere.

- **Get Creative.** As Thomas Edison famously said, "There's always a better way." If you find a real barrier does exist, start by figuring out your goal. Let your imagination work backwards to see if other solutions present themselves. In my case, perhaps a protected mental downtime without phones or visitors will get me close to the same result as a nap for now.

- **Take Baby Steps.** If you find you can move forward where you are, don't hesitate to start small. But do start. As Michael Hyatt has said, "Motion leads to momentum." Maybe you can't do it all right away, but you can do something. Sit down. Jot down a plan. Take steps, even small ones, in the right direction. Do it today.

- **Keep Moving Forward.** These three words from one of my life leaders, Walt Disney, sum it up. William H. Murray added this wisdom that I have found true again and again: "The moment one definitely commits oneself ... all sorts of things occur to help one that would never have otherwise occurred." Unlike the rides at Walt's magical World, we should always refuse to come to a complete stop.

Above all, know that you've got a lot of friends here who feel your growth pains when you hit a wall. I can't be the only one. Let's cheer each other on—after our naps, of course.

What walls are you hitting at this stage of your growth? How can we help each other get over them? You can leave a comment by clicking here.

The post begins with **Attention**, pulling in the reader who was intrigued by the idea of taking naps and wanted to do it. However, that reader likely also experienced the **Tension** of trying to work naps into their daily schedule.

As I described the Tension, I made a **Connection** from my own experience and efforts to find fresh ways to keep growing even if I couldn't do exactly what was recommended—take a nap.

Most of the post then unpacks the **Solution** I propose so the reader can also overcome that wall to their personal growth.

Finally, I reinforce the **Connection** and then invite readers to take **Action** by leaving a comment and engaging in the discussion about it.

This example is a simple one to demonstrate how The StoryTelling Structure™ flows at a high level. We'll unpack more in the chapters to come. For now, note that although the post follows a structure (the science), it doesn't feel formulaic; it feels free (the art).

You can even see The StoryTelling Structure™ in the flow of this very chapter. Take a peek back through the last few pages and see if you can identify the different elements. Go ahead and flip back. I'll wait.

Okay. Did you find them? No doubt the easiest one to find was **Attention.** Hopefully, the references to classic Disney stories felt familiar as they tapped into what you wanted—a simple way to tell your story and share your message with the world.

But there was a problem, wasn't there? It was the **Tension** of the dreaded storyteller's enemy, "call it writer's block, the blinking cursor, or the blank page."

Not to worry. I feel your pain. I spent my Saturdays at the library doing nerdy things and decades studying and writing so you don't have to. You are correct: That's the **Connection.**

Then I shared the **Solution**: Follow The StoryTelling Structure™ to solve your problem and get what you want.

See? Far from feeling forced, the use of *science* to structure your story frees you to focus on the *art* of communicating.

Now it's time for you to take **Action.**

YOUR ADVANTAGE ACTIVITIES

What went through your head the last time you had to write something longer than a text message? Did it feel stressful or taxing? Or did you hand it off to someone else? (No judgment here if you did.)

Even though I love writing, a lot of people don't. The problem is that they still have stories to tell, so the challenge then becomes getting over the anxiety of writing. That's where The StoryTelling Structure™ will save you.

Either in your head, in your journal, or in the space below, practice using the structure to share your Meaningful Message from Chapter 1.

1. Attention. If you were telling someone about your Meaningful Message or story, how would you grab their Attention? What do they really want?

2. Tension. What's keeping them from getting that thing? What problem is holding them back?

3. Connection. When have you experienced that same problem? How did you come out the other side and achieve the goal or gain the thing? What credentials would you share as evidence of your success?

4.Solution. What are the steps someone would need to take to solve their problem and get what they want using your proven process? What did you do to solve it?

5. Action. What do you most want them to do after hearing your Meaningful Message? Take specific action? Connect with you for support? Book you to speak?

How did thinking through those questions just now make you feel? Don't judge it on whether it's good or bad for now. I'll show you how to keep shaping it in the chapters to come.

The Message Maker:
Your BrandStory

Muniba Mazari had been traveling through rural Pakistan to her family's home in Rahim Yar Khan to celebrate her twenty-first birthday when her car careened through the metal railing that separated the road from a steep ditch.

People nearby rushed to her aid, pulling a bleeding and broken Muniba from the wreckage of the vehicle. With no emergency medical care in the area, she was laid in the back of a waiting Jeep and driven to the nearest clinic that was willing to try to treat her extensive injuries.

A young, newly married Pakistani woman ready to start her life as a wife, mother, and artist, Muniba received devastating news. She would never walk again, and she could never carry a child. And due to extensive damage to the nerves and bones in her right hand, becoming an artist was out of the question. Her doctor told her she would need Plan B. But she didn't have one.

Muniba spent her birthday in the intensive care unit, surrounded by flowers from people wishing her happiness and a speedy recovery. She was in the best hospital in Karachi, living through the worst days of her life. Everything she had dreamed about and planned seemed no longer possible. And frankly, life no longer felt worth living.

With the enormity of the situation pressing on her heart and mind, Muniba broke down in tears. Her mother simply held her and said, "One day you will be shown why you were chosen for this test."

For nearly two years, Muniba moved in and out of the hospital as her body healed from broken bones, continuous infections, and deep pressure sores. When she was finally able to sit in a wheelchair and see herself in a full-length mirror for the first time, she didn't recognize the hollowed-out, paraplegic woman before her. But through it all, she picked up her brush and began pouring her heart and pain out onto a canvas, processing her lost future one stroke at a time.

As the years passed, Muniba began to discover the purpose behind her pain. As people came and went in her life, many things she had once been told were impossible actually started to become realities. Although she was wheelchair-bound, she adopted a baby and became a mother. She painted and exhibited her artwork in galleries, earning a living from selling them. She got her first job outside the home and opened her first bank account.

Then TEDx in Islamabad called. The people there had seen her art and inspiring social media posts and wanted her to come and speak.

Even though Muniba had never given a speech before, she found the courage to face the crowd and tell her story—the terrible accident that left her paralyzed, the grueling physical recovery, and the even tougher emotional recovery. She shared her struggles and triumphs and what losing the use of her legs had taught her about empathy and compassion. She knew her story could help other people.

After Muniba shared her story, a young woman approached her in tears to thank her. Hearing how Muniba had overcome so much gave the young woman strength and confidence to get

Your story is about you, but your story isn't for you.

through her own tough things too. That's when it hit Muniba: Her story was *about* her, but it wasn't *for* her. Telling her story gave strength, hope, courage, and perspective to others and allowed them to find ways to process their own struggles.

And that's exactly what you need to know: Your story is *about* you, but your story isn't *for* you.

WHY YOU SHOULD GET INTENTIONAL

Whether you are thinking of your personal story or your organizational story, it's natural that you might think it should focus on you. After all it is *your* story. But as the steward of your story, the first thing to know is that it is for the people you serve, your audience, or your customers. That means you need to tell your story in a way that resonates with the people you want to reach, which may not be the way you want to hear it.

Figuring out who your story is for is a critical piece of the initial phase of discovering your Story EcoSystem™—your BrandStory.

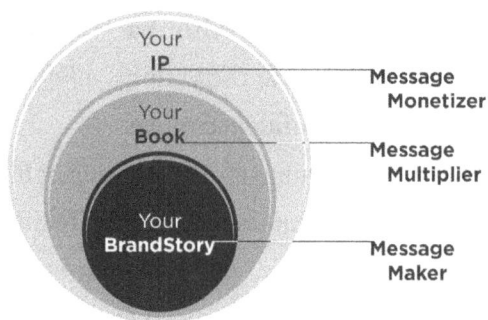

This initial Message Maker phase is all about developing three things in your story: clarity, simplicity, and connectivity. You need it to be so clear that it cannot be misunderstood, so simple that anyone can get it, and so easy to connect with that your audience can't help but be drawn to you. That's why your focus in this phase should be on crafting what I call your BrandStory. Your BrandStory is a dynamic document that conveys your story and message in a way that resonates with your core audience.

Without it, communication for either your personal brand or your organization can become scattered as different people describe your mission in different ways. When your story gets told or your message is shared, even by your own team, the messenger reinvents it rather than simply using the copy-and-paste language you want them to use. Thus, the BrandStory frees you and your team to focus on moving your message forward instead of continually remaking it—just as a proven storytelling structure frees your mind to be more creative.

Whether your brand is you as an individual or for your organization, at the most basic level it is simply how you present and talk about who you are to the rest of the world. Unfortunately, most people don't get intentional about sharing their story with the world. They just let whatever happens, happen. As a result, they lose control of their own story.

For people who have experienced some success before getting intentional about their story, a different problem arises: distraction. While being in demand may be good for their business or brand, it can be easy to get busy doing the work in front of them instead of thinking about telling the story their audience or customers want and need to hear. Then the business starts to plateau because they focus on doing more of the same things instead of telling their story well and breaking through to the next level.

With the rise of social media, I've seen a third situation arise. Too many people unintentionally introduce friction into their message by talking about all sorts of things on their public and personal accounts, creating disconnect in the process. They're so busy posting about what they want to talk about *in the moment* that they include elements that feel out of place to their audience. This is partly due to the person neither being sure who their audience is nor understanding what that audience needs from them. This friction then causes them to work harder than they need to without getting the results they want—and they can't understand why.

All these scenarios result in limited impact, influence, and income.

The difference between a poor BrandStory and a great BrandStory is the first gap that keeps people from achieving the impact, influence, and income they desire. The following chart shows a few of the differences between the two.

THE BRANDSTORY GAP CHART

Poor	Great
Scattered: You haven't narrowed down what you do well.	**Focused:** You have an intentional message that shares what you do.
General: You're trying to reach everyone, so you're reaching no one.	**Specific:** Your message is distinct and narrowed to your audience.
You-focused: You think only about what you want to say instead of what others need to hear.	**Audience-focused:** You think strategically and share about what your audience wants to hear.
Confusing: Your message is cluttered and doesn't make sense.	**Clear:** Your message is simple and easy to understand.
Wordy: Your message is too detailed and in the weeds.	**Concise:** You say what needs to be said and nothing more.
Forgettable: You haven't found what makes you distinct and how to say it.	**Sticky:** You tell your message in a way that's memorable and usable.
Random: There's no common thread in what you're saying, so it's hard for others to share your story.	**Repeatable:** Your message is easy for others to remember and share.

Creating a great BrandStory is the first step toward increasing your impact, influence, and income. If you want to grow, you must get intentional about the story you're telling.

When I was initially creating the groundwork for StoryBuilders, I had many conversations in which I shared

If you want to grow, you must get intentional about the story you're telling.

my dream of what the company would be, but I didn't have complete clarity yet. That lack of clarity made it difficult to explain it to others. For many years, my own family told me they weren't sure what I did. I would start to talk about it, and five minutes later, I'd still be talking—and they would still be confused.

I knew that in order to succeed, I had to get clear and speak in a way that would connect with people. I had to get more concise and create messaging that was sticky and memorable. I had to speak in a way that allowed my target audience to find me and connect with me.

There's a common saying: "If I had more time, I'd write a shorter letter." It takes work to make a message more concise and intentional. As I continued to develop language for who StoryBuilders was and what we did, I worked through a process similar to the one we now follow for creating a BrandStory using The StoryTelling Structure™. I spent time digging into my origin story and finding my own why, which helped me figure out who we could best serve.

Now when people ask what we do, I say, "We tell stories that make the world a better place because we believe every story matters. We do that by helping entrepreneurs, business professionals, and thought leaders elevate their messages to create memorable brand stories, compelling books, and engaging learning experiences that maximize impact, influence, and income."

The Story Telling Structure®

With BrandStory Addition

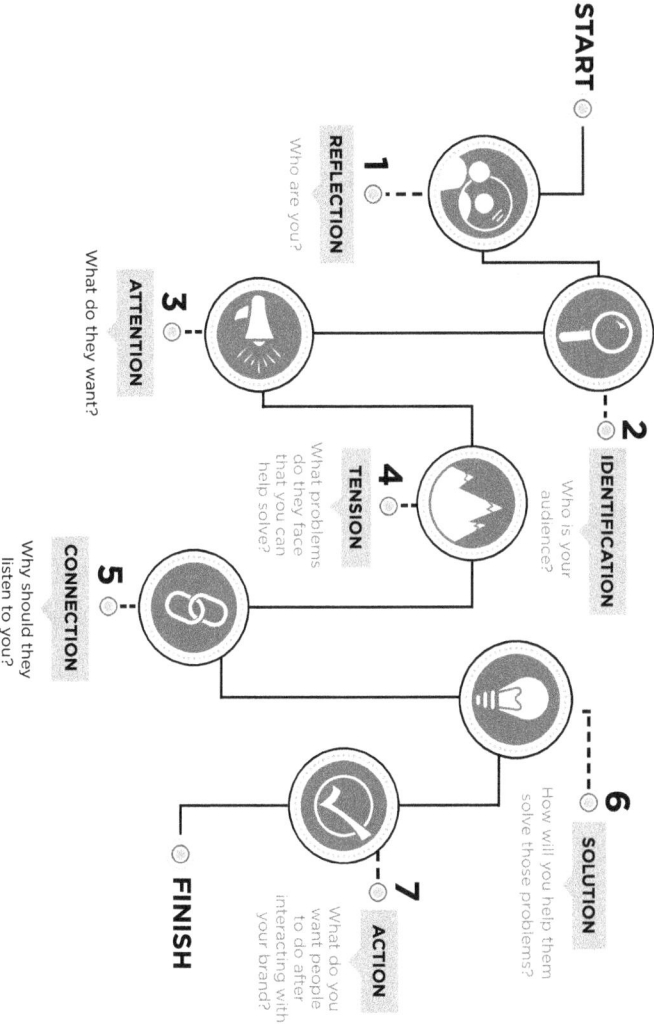

START

1 REFLECTION
Who are you?

2 IDENTIFICATION
Who is your audience?

3 ATTENTION
What do they want?

4 TENSION
What problems do they face that you can help solve?

5 CONNECTION
Why should they listen to you?

6 SOLUTION
How will you help them solve those problems?

7 ACTION
What do you want people to do after interacting with your brand?

FINISH

45

THE BRANDSTORY PROCESS

The BrandStory process expands on The StoryTelling Structure™ introduced in the last chapter. It simply adds two foundational elements to the beginning—Reflection and Identification—and goes deeper on all the other elements.

Let's dive in and see how it works.

Step 1. Reflection. *Who are you … really?*

Few people pause to reflect on who they are. After all, they know themselves, so what is there to reflect on? The reality is that it is hard work to get to know yourself. And it is so easy to get distracted doing other things that it seems less important to figure out who we are, which means we never really do. Ironically, we take ourselves for granted and never invest the time to get clear on who we are. We can live just fine without that knowledge, though. Right? Maybe. But no one else can ever really know who you are unless you tell them your story. And believe me, that will become an issue in your growth at some point, if it hasn't already.

This Reflection phase forces us to ask, *who am I?* Simon Sinek's classic work *Start with Why* challenged readers not to start with what they do or even describe how they do it but to begin with *why* they do what they

Your why must be authentic to who you are.

do. I agree that our *why* trumps both our *what* and our *how* and positions us to better connect with our audience. However, there's more to it—a deeper level beneath the *why* that we must get clear on, and here's the reason.

Your *why* must be authentic to *who* you are. Think about it. No one ever picked their *why* out of thin air. No one ever woke up one morning and randomly said, "My *why* is to ensure everyone in the world has fresh, clean water to drink." If that is their *why*, I guarantee it came from somewhere deeper—the story of who they are. Maybe somewhere along the way, they saw the impact of not having fresh water and were moved to do something about it. Maybe their childhood was shaped by living in poverty and lacking life's essentials, and now they want to ensure no one else has to endure what they did. Their *why* flowed naturally from *who* they are— and that is true for all of us. Our *why*, if it is authentic, flows from *who* we are.

In my own journey, I've always had a passion for storytelling, reading stories, and writing stories. So it's no surprise that my authentic *why* is to help people tell stories. It's also not surprising that the *why* of StoryBuilders expands on it. Because we believe every story matters, we tell stories that make the world a better place.

None of us really start with *why*. We start with *who*. *Why* and *what* we do flow naturally from *who* we are. Getting clear on *who* we are empowers us to tell our stories in a way that resonates with others. It gives us confidence to know where our *why* comes from and positions us to share our stories in a way that can truly resonate with the people we want to connect with the most.

Another reason we should start with *who* instead of *why* is consistency. As you build a team around you, whether as a personal brand or across your organization, you want everyone to tell the same story. You want to share the same clear message every time and in every place.

In the iconic ride at Disney World, "it's a small world" (Walt made it all lower case), all the doll children sing the same song in every room. (Yes, I have been stuck in boat traffic on that ride many times.) As a result, you don't leave thinking you just heard scores of different countries all telling their own unique stories. You leave whistling one single tune: "It's a small world after all."

That's what you want for your own team—everyone singing the same song, telling the same story, and using the same words to describe *who* you are, *why* you do *what* you do, and *how* you do what you do. But it all begins with *who*.

When you tell that founding story well to your internal team, they feel connected to its source.

This Reflection phase should include a deeper telling of your origin story as well. By origin story, I mean *how* you got started doing *what* you're doing and *how* the company you founded came to be, *what* it is today, and *how* the team you lead began and grew. As organizations grow and time passes, it's easy to lose sight of the origin story and thus lose touch with the founding mission. But when you tell that founding story well to your internal team, they feel connected to its source. They feel a greater sense of belonging to a larger mission, and they are equipped to tell that origin story to your audience or customers.

Think about some of the iconic brands you may encounter on a daily basis. They became iconic because they've told the story of *who* they are and *why* they do *what* they do in a way that resonated with their audiences. Chick-fil-A has its famous cows telling people to "eat mor chikin"—the mainstay the famous restaurant chain created when it was still a small diner in Georgia. But more than that, the name of the business says it all: Chick-fil-A is short for "chicken fillet" with the "A" highlighting the quality customers can expect.[2] And the best part is that you see this story on the walls of every franchise you visit. Its story is central to who the company is, and people are willing to pay more for its service because of it.

That's *why* we created the BrandStory Bundle at StoryBuilders. We found that businesses often didn't talk about their origin stories. Over time, they often got overlooked and even forgotten, a missed opportunity to connect with team members and customers alike on a deeper level. Our BrandStory Bundle includes not only the dynamic BrandStory, the touchstone document for outward-facing messaging to reach your ideal customers, but also a compelling telling of the origin story for your brand or organization. It creatively shares your core values and equips your team for maximum buy-in of who you are.

This Reflection phase is also where your Meaningful Message typically comes to life, or rather where your message becomes meaningful because it is clearly connected to *who* you are. For example, my Meaningful Message ("Every story matters") clearly stems from *who* I am and fuels StoryBuilders' mission to serve our StoryPartners by telling their stories well.

Your story doesn't have to be a long treatise; it can be as short as a couple of paragraphs, a half page, or a full page. If you go back to Chapter 1, you'll see that my story was a total of about a page and a half. However, your origin story might be longer and can serve as the foundation for an entire book or booklet, which includes your Meaningful Message.

Step 2. Identification. *Who is your audience?*

Once you're clear on who you are, the next obvious question becomes this: *Who is your audience?* Who do you really want to serve? My friend Rory Vaden, the *New York Times* bestselling author and cofounder of Brand Builders Group, puts it this way: "You are most perfectly positioned to serve the person you once were."[3]

Reflecting on who you are already gives you an advantage at this stage. When you know yourself, you are most ready to know your audience. Perhaps you have developed a personal or professional brand that is all about helping the person you once were, and that puts you closer to having a great BrandStory. Most of us, though, need to spend more time defining that audience.

Even if you think you already know who your audience is, I would recommend reviewing it to make sure it's still accurate. I'm always amazed at how few organizations take the time to identify who their customers, donors, and stakeholders truly are. It's a rewarding exercise that will help you define your space in your market, bringing to life the old adage that the person who aims at nothing will surely hit it.

So who is your audience? Who are those people for you?

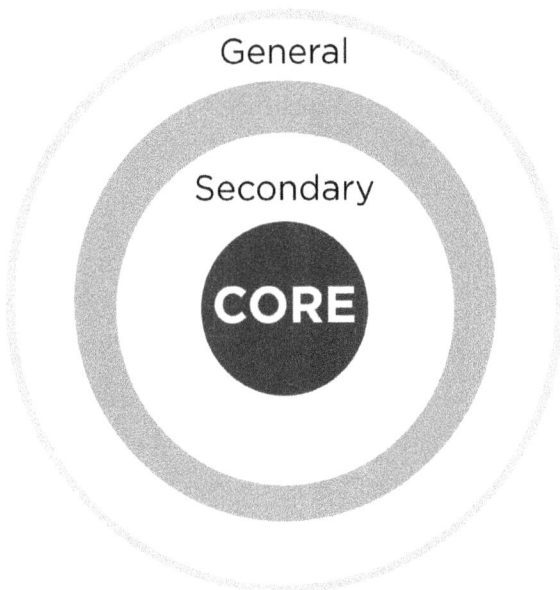

General

Secondary

CORE

It may help to think about your audience as three concentric circles. In the first circle are your core people—they align the most with your message and connect most deeply with your story. They are your target audience and primary focus. You must identify and clearly focus on them.

The secondary audience is the next larger circle beyond your core. These are people who will probably be drawn to your message as you tell your story to your core audience. They're not your core audience, but they might become your core audience or are related to or connected with your core audience in some way. While they're not your primary focus, they are a valid secondary audience that you should be aware of and perhaps acknowledge in your storytelling and message sharing.

Don't try to tell your story in a way that will appeal to everybody.

Finally, there is the broader audience of people with whom your story *may* resonate and who *may* eventually do business with you, connect with you, or support your organization. But either the timing isn't right yet or they probably are not a great fit. These people may be great people, but they should not be the focus of your BrandStory. People often get this wrong and try to reach that general audience instead of the core audience, thinking that more is necessarily better. When they do this, they end up diluting their original message to the core audience, sometimes to the point where the core audience no longer identifies with them. When this happens, they begin to lose brand clarity and distinction, and introduce unwanted friction.

Don't try to tell your story in a way that will appeal to everybody. Instead, focus your energy, resources, and messaging on your core audience, invite your secondary audience into a process to become your core audience, and be aware of the general audience that might at least talk about you to others.

Step 3. Attention. *What does your audience want... really?*

As we head into Step 3, we begin to connect with the core storytelling structure that I introduced in the previous chapter. As I said, the best way to get your core audience's attention is to tap into what they want. So the question is this: *What do they want... really?*

If you know your audience well, just listen to them. Dedicating time to think about the interactions you've had with them should help give you clarity about what they really want. If you don't know them well, you can engage them with focus groups, one-on-one conversations, or even strategic surveys to fully realize what your audience wants. Whatever you do, don't simply assume. At StoryBuilders, we've done all the above at times to help our StoryPartners hone in on what their core audience wants. When you know what your core audience wants, you can get their attention by tapping into that desire.

Here's a word of caution about getting people's attention. I once had someone advise me that I should go live on social media and do something weird and zany to get people's attention as they scrolled. My response was simple: "Do you know me at all?" For those who do know me, *zany, weird,* and *crazy* are not the first words that come to their minds. It's quite the opposite. *Intentional, calm, methodical,* and maybe even *cerebral* describe me better. While there certainly can be a place for doing outlandish things from time to time to break through the noise, you want to be careful that you don't get someone's attention by being inauthentic to who you are. If you were to come across a video of me doing something wacky online and be drawn in by it, you might then be disappointed to learn that's not my usual approach. So while I may have attracted you, I haven't done it in an authentic way, and thus I've already broken trust with you at the beginning of the relationship.

Whatever your natural style is or whatever the voice of your brand is, be sure you're getting people's attention in a way that's consistent with who you are—like cows holding signs telling people to "eat mor chickin."

Step 4. Tension. *What's keeping them from getting what they want... really?*

Your personal brand, business, or organization exists to solve a problem of some sort. Don't run from that. Lean into it and embrace the tension. Once you know what your audience wants, ask what's holding them back from getting what they want. What's stopping them from already having it?

The answer to that question may require a little digging. For example, if you run a business, you might be tempted to say, "The reason people don't buy my product or service is that they don't have enough money. That's what's keeping them from what they want." But as any good salesperson will tell you, money is almost never the reason people don't buy. There's always more to it.

You have to be willing and able to go deeper. You want to know the *tangible* tension, the physical barriers that stop people—a lack of money, time, information, or other things that can be touched or measured. But you also want to know about the deeper *intangible* tensions—the fears, concerns, anxieties, and deeper psychological burdens that keep them awake at night. For example, someone may tell you they simply don't have money to buy your product or service, but what really might be holding them back is a fear that they aren't good enough to deserve it. The *tangible* tension about money is really driven by a deeper *intangible* tension around self-worth.

The Meaningful Message you began to work on in the Reflection step should come back into play here. There should be a connection between this Tension step and your Meaningful Message, which should be something that resonates with the people who are struggling through this tension. For example, someone might say, "I want to maximize my impact, influence, and income, and work with experts to help tell my story well, but I don't know that the timing is right." However, beneath that concern about timing may be a self-confidence struggle or a fear of failure or rejection. When that's the case, your story can tap into that core belief of our Meaningful Message—every story matters. Deep down, they know that's true. Then it's just a matter of helping them see how their story, when told well, can indeed make the world a better place and multiply their impact, influence, and income in the process.

If you discover that your Meaningful Message just doesn't seem to align with the Tension you know your audience wrestles with, it may signal a disconnect. Perhaps what you think is your Meaningful Message really isn't your Meaningful Message. Perhaps your audience is out of focus, you haven't really tapped into what they want, or you don't truly understand their problems.

If it feels like there is a disconnect, I encourage you to circle back and review the first four steps. And if you need help, just reach out.

Step 5. Connection. *Why should they listen to you?*

Given that your audience has these problems they want to overcome, why should they listen to you? How can you demonstrate that you understand those problems and have found a way to overcome them?

Remember that although your story is *about* you, it isn't *for* you. This step establishes a link between you and your audience. The link happens when you

A little vulnerability goes a long way.

share your message in a way that connects the Tension they feel with your experiences and expertise. In other words, it's now time to share about you.

The first thing they need to know is that you understand how it feels to have the problems they have. If your audience is the person you once were, then you are perfectly positioned to share your story as evidence that you do indeed "get it." At this step, a little vulnerability goes a long way. You may think that you need to tell the world you are perfect and always have been, but sharing your struggles and failures lets your audience know you've "been there, done that" just like them. And if you could do it, maybe they can too. When you lean into being open about your struggles, you open the door for authentic connection and trust.

The second thing you want them to know is that you didn't stay stuck in the struggle. You found a way forward. You experienced success, and you can show them how to do the same thing. In other words, this is your moment to brag. Go ahead. You don't get many of these moments in life, so lean into this one. Don't hold back. Lay it all out and clean it up later by sorting through what's important or not important to your audience. Illustrate to them that you in fact have found a way forward—and have the credentials to prove it.

Surprisingly, many people take their experience for granted. For example, if a family business has been doing what it's been doing for sixty-five years, it may be easy to gloss over that and simply say, "Oh yeah, we've been doing this for a while. We know everything there is to know about that." But staying in business for sixty-five years is a big deal. Taking the time to unpack the value of those sixty-five years lets people know you've seen and done it all and still succeeded. Perhaps a business might add certifications, accreditations, or other success credentials. Or it might add financial data to show market share or industry brand dominance—whatever would move the trust needle most for the audience.

If you are an individual thought leader or business professional, then your credentials might include time invested in a specific industry gaining your expertise, education, or other outside accreditations and additional benchmarks like books published, sales made, or speeches given and to whom. Whatever the data might be to demonstrate your expertise, share it here to show you know what you are doing.

Of all the BrandStory parts, this one can and should feel more like a checklist than others, but it's essential to give yourself the credibility to present your audience with the next step—the solution.

Step 6. Solution. *How will you help them ... exactly?*

The people we work with have wisdom and insights for solving specific problems in a wide variety of areas. I'm always amazed by the depth of their creativity and expertise, and the solutions they offer to their audiences, and how scattered those solutions can be.

They have part of a valuable message here and a little bit over there. But they struggle to organize it all in a sticky and memorable way that is unique to them. One of the greatest values we bring when working with a person or team is that we gather all those parts into a unique order and method. You may have better ideas or processes than someone else, but if that someone else can communicate with greater clarity, your audience will probably listen to them instead of you. It's that simple.

The challenge so many creatives face is that they have no shortage of great ideas. It goes back to The Creativity Conundrum I talked about in Chapter 1. The more creative ideas you have, the harder it becomes to get any of them done. But if you're going to clarify your BrandStory, you have to be willing to do two things.

> The more creative ideas you have, the harder it becomes to get any of them done.

First, you must be willing to kill your darlings. That is, you must be willing to let go of ideas, services, or messages that may be meaningful to you but do not resonate with your audience. For example, I double majored in college. Along with English, I studied history because I find it rich with stories and examples of every kind. If I need to illustrate a point, I often look to the past. But sometimes I can overdo it. For example, once when working with a well-known thought leader's team, I tried to bring a certain leadership principle to life. I reached into my history vault and thought of how General Lee made decisions on the field during the Battle of Gettysburg. In trying to tell the story, though, it quickly became apparent that I had lost everybody in the room in the tactical weeds. So, even though I liked the story and thought it illustrated the concept well, I let it slide back into history for the sake of clarity. What should have been a simple leadership principle was obscured by all the historical nuances, so it had to go. (Our team still laughs about how I tried so hard to make that story work.)

Second, you have to simplify your solution. You may have a process you follow to help people resolve the tensions they face and achieve what they want, but if you haven't done the work to make it understandable and accessible to your audience, there's a good chance most of them won't use it. Thus, they won't solve their problems, and you won't accomplish your mission.

You must be willing to simplify, simplify, simplify. As U.S. Supreme Court Justice Oliver Wendell Holmes said, "For the simplicity on this side of complexity, I wouldn't give you a fig. But for the simplicity on the other side of complexity, for that

I would give you anything I have." You may not want a fig, but I'll bet you do want the power of simplicity that can only come from working through the mess of ideas and complexity to reach your audience.

One famous example of simplicity on the other side of complexity is John C. Maxwell's signature solution for leadership growth, *The 5 Levels of Leadership*. Sure, Maxwell has written a lot of wise things about leadership, but all of it fits into that simple paradigm for understanding leadership itself.

Likewise, Stephen R. Covey simplified extensive personal growth wisdom into his classic *The 7 Habits of Highly Effective People*. You don't need to know everything—just follow these seven simple habits to succeed. The point is that once you do the challenging work of simplifying the process, it becomes sticky, repeatable, and shareable.

Once you land on your process and simplify it, it's time to name it. Marketing guru Seth Godin describes the value of naming your solution this way: "Naming permits us to store it, work on it, and talk about it." Naming brings your solution to life in a tangible way, and it makes it possible for you to tell your friends, clients, or coworkers about it. It makes it possible for *them* to tell others about you too.

> "Naming permits us to store it, work on it, and talk about it." — Seth Godin.

When we worked with a multi-generational family business that excelled at repairing chimneys, we helped them define the process they go through to provide the solution of chimney repair. We then gave that solution a name. In defining the process, we helped simplify the language so their customers weren't overwhelmed with all the details. Certainly, if someone wanted more information, the technician could walk them through the nitty-gritty details (literally), but the business found that most people weren't interested in *how* a chimney was repaired. They just wanted to know the company had a proven process for getting the job done. Naming it made it easier for everyone.

When naming your solution, align the name with what your audience wants so the outcome is clear. If your business offers a speedy oil change, you probably don't want to call your solution the Butterfly Tooth Cleaning Tool (actually, I haven't checked YouTube; it might be a thing.) But you may want to use something like the 10-Minute Oil Change (I know, Pennzoil has already used that one.) The customer who wants a speedy oil change knows there is a process for delivering what they want. On the other hand, if you are into butterfly dentistry, the first option may be the best name for you.

You get the idea. Name your Solution, but align it with what your audience wants.

Here's one final thought: As you develop your solution, consider what may feel normal to you versus what is normal for your customer. Think about what information they need in order to make the right decision for their problem without overwhelming them with nomenclature and twenty-seven steps. They already have enough on their plate. By simplifying your process and naming it, you eliminate the weight of finding a specific solution while demonstrating to them that you are here to serve them, you understand their fears, *and* you can solve their problems.

Step 7. Action. *What is the next best step to take?*

I once had the privilege of working with the messages of the great communicator Zig Ziglar. I watched countless hours of Zig teaching on everything from personal growth to the art of selling. I'll share more about that later, but one thing that stuck with me from his sales presentation was the critical importance of actually asking for the sale.

You have to ask for what you want. Some of us might not feel comfortable doing that for any number of reasons, but when we view the Solution we offer

You have to ask for what you want.

to our audience as something that can truly help them, why would we not intentionally invite them to experience the benefits that come from embracing it?

On the other hand, if we really don't believe our solution can help them, perhaps we should reconsider what we're doing in the first place. However, if you've made it this far in this book, I'd say there's a very good chance you have a message worth sharing with the world, and it will make the world a better place *if* you invite people to act.

This phase of the BrandStory will vary depending on the context. If someone is experiencing your story on your website, the action you might want them to take is "Click to Buy" a product or "Connect for a Conversation." If you're sharing your story on a sales call, the action you might invite them to take is to enroll in your program or invest in your opportunity. On the other hand, if you're posting on social media, the action may be to like, share, or subscribe. The context will determine the action, but you still have to ask for the action. Make sure it is clear and easy to understand and do.

That, in a nutshell, is the process for creating a great BrandStory. Your BrandStory can then be used as the touchstone for all the communication for your brand, from websites to email, from advertising to social media descriptions, and from books to masterclasses.

Here's an idea of what to expect as you create your own BrandStory. When we create a BrandStory with our StoryPartners, the full version typically runs anywhere from ten to twenty pages. We also create a condensed one- to two-page version and an even more concise "elevator pitch" version for easy sharing. Here is StoryBuilders' own version: "We believe every story matters. That's why we tell stories that make the world a better place. We do that by helping entrepreneurs, business professionals, and thought leaders elevate their message. We create memorable brand stories, compelling books, and engaging learning experiences to maximize impact, influence, and income."

Earlier I said that your BrandStory is a dynamic document. By dynamic, I mean it will grow and change as you do. This isn't a one-and-done moment. That doesn't mean it should change all the time, but it will need to adapt and grow as you do. As a general rule, it's a good idea to revisit your BrandStory every year to see what adjustments you might need to make.

This Message Maker phase creates a clear, simple, and cohesive foundation for your Story EcoSystem™. The next phase builds on the story to provide you with the Message Multiplier.

YOUR ADVANTAGE ACTIVITIES

As I've said throughout this chapter, your message needs to be clear. It needs to be simple. And it needs to connect with your audience. While it will take some time to create a great BrandStory from scratch, if you're reading this book, chances are you already have some semblance of a BrandStory for your business.

For the sake of this simple exercise, let's walk through how you could revise your existing BrandStory using the seven steps outlined above. Choose how to answer based on whether you are building your personal brand or a business or organizational brand.

1. Reflection: Who are you ... really? At your core? What do you deeply value? What do you want to accomplish that really matters to you?

2. Identification: Who is your audience or customer? Who are you best positioned to serve? It could be simple like "hungry people" in the case of a restaurant, or it could be deeper like "young entrepreneurs trying to balance life and work."

3. Attention: What does your audience want ... really? Your audience may want a good meal for a reasonable price. They're hungry, they're busy, and they work hard. But why do they want that? In the case of young entrepreneurs, they may want help figuring out how to build a successful business without sacrificing time with their family. But why does that matter to them? Be willing to go deep here to explore what really motivates the people you want to reach.

4. Tension: What's keeping them from getting what they want? Why can't they satiate their hunger? Maybe they don't have time to leave the office, and they're not good at preparing a lunch to bring with them (tangible problem). *And* maybe they don't feel like they can take a break to eat because they already have too much on their metaphorical plates (intangible problem). Why can't young entrepreneurs find balance? Maybe they don't have a grasp of the right tools that could help bring balance to their lives (tangible problem). Maybe they see their successful peers sacrificing their personal lives and think that if they aren't willing to sacrifice everything, they won't be good enough to succeed (intangible problem).

5. Connection: Why should they listen to you? How did you encounter and solve this problem? How can you let them know you've felt their pain and found a better way?

6. Solution: How will you help them exactly? What solution to their problem do you offer? What process do you suggest they follow? What do you suggest they do and in what order? (Examples: "30 Minutes or It's Free" lunch specials; the Entrepreneur's Energy Engine.)

7. Action: What is the next best step to take? What do you want them to do next? Stop in for your thirty-minute lunch special? Download your app? Enlist your coaching services? What action should they take to move closer to getting what they really want?

If you want more support to act
on what you learn in this book, visit
YourStoryAdvantage.com/FreeResources or scan the
QR code to discover FREE resources to help you
maximize your story.

4

The Message
Multiplier: Your Book

lenn was only seven years old when he set out to walk two miles to school one winter morning in 1916. Along with his two brothers and sister, he hurried across the frozen ground from their humble home on the plains of Kansas to the empty, wooden, one-room schoolhouse.

Glenn and his thirteen-year-old older brother, Floyd, went to prepare the room for the day as their younger sister and brother played outside on the swings. But once they entered the building, the door latch dropped into place, preventing anyone else from coming in.

As Floyd began stirring up the coals in the fireplace, Glenn shuffled over to the chalkboard to draw. Fortunately, the teacher kept a can of kerosene near the mantel to help start the fire that heated the large room, and the children were trained to safely light the wood. But on this morning, as Floyd held a burning match to the wood, Glenn smelled the distinctive odor of not kerosene but gasoline.

In an instant, the gasoline fumes exploded, blowing the boys across the room as everything burst into flames. Their siblings outside raced to the door, only to find it latched from within. Still in shock from the explosion, the boys inside stumbled blindly toward the door. After fumbling with the latch while flames raced over them, they opened the door and stumbled out into the winter cold, frantically looking for snow on the frozen dirt.

Desperate to put out the flames, they rolled on the frozen ground. Once the flames were out, the shock set in. They were two miles from home and had second- and third-degree burns over most of their bodies, but they started to run toward their house with their siblings chasing after them.

For two miles, they ran, stumbled, fell, and staggered forward. Finally, they collapsed in front of their home, only to remember that no one was home. Unable to move any farther, the two injured boys writhed on the ground in agony as their sister ran to their closest neighbor for help.

When the children's parents and a doctor finally arrived, it was clear that both boys had suffered horrific burns. But out there on the prairie, the only thing the doctor could do was clean the wounds and pray. He told the parents not to expect either of the boys to survive, and within a few weeks, Floyd did succumb to his injuries.

Meanwhile, Glenn's legs were burned so badly, he could no longer walk, yet his mother refused to give up on him. For the next year and half, Glenn stayed in bed, praying that his muscles and skin would heal.

When Glenn turned nine, his parents managed to get him out of bed. At first he could only stand for thirty seconds at a time while holding onto a chair. With practice and perseverance, he moved from the chair to the door to outside. His father bound his hands to a cart and walked him slowly forward, forcing his legs to relearn how to walk.

Eventually, the boy began to jog—and then even run. He staggered at first but never quit trying. Sometime later, he began running to and from school each day and alongside his family's cart when they went into town. He soon became known throughout the town as "the boy who wouldn't stop running."

When Glenn reached high school in the early 1920s, he joined the track team and began shattering records. His coach unofficially clocked him running a mile in less than four minutes—something that had never been done before. The barrier that everyone had said couldn't be broken was shattered by a boy who was told he would never walk again.

For the next fifteen years, Glenn Cunningham was known as the fastest miler in the world. At the 1932 Olympics, he was favored to win the gold medal. However, he came down with tonsillitis a few days before the event and had to pull out. But he didn't stop. He returned four years later and won a silver medal in the 1936 Berlin Olympics.

That's a great story. But here's the thing: The only reason I know it and can share it with you is because I read about it in a book Glenn wrote called *Never Quit*. I'm not even sure how it came into my possession. It has a handwritten note in it from someone who knew Glenn personally. They gave it to someone who gave it to someone—and somehow it ended up in my hands. And his story found its way into my heart.

> **A book can go places you will never go and touch more people than you will ever know.**

Glenn Cunningham never could have predicted his book would have fallen into my hands, and yet it did. Not only have I been inspired by his story, but my children have also heard it. Students I taught for years and attendees at events where I have spoken for the last decade have heard it too. But I never could have shared Glenn's story if he hadn't written a book. The book multiplied his message. And even more powerful for me is knowing that Glenn didn't write the book himself. He had a collaborative writer (someone like me and our StoryBuilders team) who helped him tell his story well.

Glenn couldn't have predicted the details of his book's impact, but its path is not unusual. That's why I call a book your Message Multiplier. A book can go places you will never go and touch more people than you will ever know.

WHAT YOUR BOOK CAN DO FOR YOU

A book serves as a force multiplier for your message, a powerful lever that can elevate your story in many unique ways. The ancient mathematician Archimedes once said, "Give me a lever long enough and a fulcrum on which to place it, and I shall move the world." Think of your book as an extension of your Influence Lever—long enough to move more than you ever could on your own to share your message with the world.

Without a book, you may apply a lot of effort (the thick arrow in the illustration below), but all your considerable effort can only move your message so far out to the world because your lever simply isn't long enough.

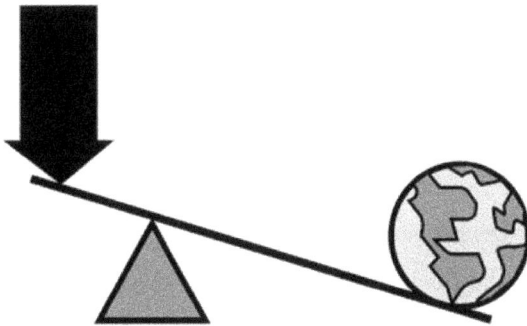

With a book, however, your leverage grows exponentially. Your story then moves farther with less effort, taking your potential impact on the world with it.

Here are just a few ways books serve to extend your influence lever.

1. **Your Expert Credential.** When you have written a book, people presume you are an expert on that topic as you have, quite literally, written the book about it. The truth is that you probably are that expert due to the time and learning invested in creating the content for the book. For many of our StoryPartners, the book flows out of what they already know as a result of doing what they do. For example, we walked alongside entrepreneur-turned-keynote-speaker Greg Cagle to write his books *Be Weird: Succeed in Life and Business Simply by Being You* and *The 4 Dimensions of Culture and the Leaders Who Shape Them.* Both books came out of his experiences building and leading companies for more than two decades. He had the knowledge, and the books shared that knowledge with the world. A book is an expert credential that opens the door

for all sorts of opportunities, including speaking and consulting.

2. **Core Content Clarifier.** Writing a book gives you clarity about the core of the content in your Story EcoSystem™. When done well, the process of putting that core knowledge—expertise, experiences, lessons, wisdom, all of it—into a book forces you to get clear on what that core content actually is, how it all fits together, and how best to talk about it with your audience. However, you could have content clarity without writing a book. For example, a speaker might use the medium of the stage to get clarity or use video to create a core message and share it. But putting all these pieces together in one place for your audience has the same effect. Crafting the cornerstone body of content, such as a book, gives the gift of clarity to you and all you reach.

3. **Business Growth Accelerator.** Perhaps it's because I like the book *10x Is Easier Than 2X* by Dan Sullivan and Dr. Benjamin Hardy that I tend to see books as a force multiplier. You can use books to grow your business in many ways, from door-opener to back-of-the-room sales to deeper conversations about doing business together. The book multiplies those opportunities and gives you an "in" to have those critical synergy-seeking

> **Books make better business cards than business cards.**

conversations. Books make better business cards than business cards since everything someone needs to know about you and your message is all together in one place. And when they finish your book, they can pass it on to another person—and another and another—which in turn opens opportunities you never could have found without it.

4. **List-Building Catalyst.** One of the most important things anyone who wants to maximize their impact, influence, and income should do is build an email list. The concept is simple: People give you permission to send them emails. If I had a nickel for every time someone said email is outdated, I'd be a billionaire by now.

The fact is, email is still the most consistent way to reach people who have given you permission to connect with them. (Texting is another tool that does something similar but has its own unique challenges.) Best of all, you are in charge of how and when you wish to send those emails, which is not the case on social media platforms where algorithms can and do change without notice. The best time to start building your list was twenty years ago. The second best time is right now ... with a book. To give value back to those people for their permission and future attention, you can offer a book or parts of a book in exchange for their email and use it in any number of creative ways to build your email list.

5. **Your Dream Converter.** Whatever your dreams may be, if you want greater impact, influence, and income, a book can help convert those dreams into reality. Not only does a book work its magic with other people, it shifts your own belief in your message and gives you the clarity and confidence to step forward boldly. When you do, who knows what might happen. As I said before, a book can go places you will never go and touch more people than you could ever imagine.

This list is not exhaustive because the possibilities for impact are endless. Think about the books that have had an impact on your own life. Which books have you read that influenced key decisions, helped you make more money, or inspired you to do bigger and better things?

Here are the five top books that have shaped my story.

1. *First Things First* by Stephen R. Covey, A. Roger Merrill, and Rebecca R. Merrill. I've read this book numerous times. It gave me the structure to get intentional about my life direction and contributed to eventually stepping into the unknown to pursue my calling.

2. *Thinking for a Change: 11 Ways Highly Successful People Approach Life and Work* by John C. Maxwell. This

isn't one of John's top sellers, but it is, in my humble opinion, one of his best. Maybe it resonated with me more because I love to think, but it did a lot to confirm the strengths I thought I had and gave me direction for how to use my unique talents.

3. *Up from Slavery* by Booker T. Washington. I read this book while I was still in school, and it stuck with me. In fact, it shaped how I approached my first job interview and how I approached tests and assignments. (I aced them both, thanks to the book.) In my humble opinion, this simple autobiography is essential reading for every person in America.

4. *10x Is Easier Than 2x: How World-Class Entrepreneurs Achieve More by Doing Less* by Dan Sullivan and Dr. Benjamin Hardy. I mentioned this book earlier in the chapter, and here's why I love it. I read this book during a key growth season, and it helped shift my thinking significantly, not only around StoryBuilders and business but life in general. It expanded my thinking about what's possible at a time when I was reorienting my own mindset in many ways.

5. *In, But Not Of: A Guide to Christian Ambition and the Desire to Influence the World* by Hugh Hewitt. This book didn't just play a pivotal role in my journey; it planted the seed long before I made the decision to step out from the school I had led for so many years.

I first read the book in 2003 while on vacation at Disney World. Due to its impact, I began teaching it to high school seniors at the school I led, and then I chose to pursue my MBA at Case Western Reserve University, one of the top programs for nonprofit leaders. This book inspired me to dream bigger. I guess it was in line with the *10x Is Easier Than 2x* book, although I hadn't given it that language over the years.

As I taught the book, I developed a curriculum to accompany it. Some years later, I met Hugh in person and pitched him the idea of pairing his book with my curriculum. He loved the idea and connected me with his publisher, with whom I became fast friends. Not coincidentally, the initial meeting with Hugh took place about nine months after the pivotal decision I mentioned in Chapter 1, the one I recorded on an index card in 2010.

The new book, which updated Hugh's content with my curriculum as a study guide, was rereleased shortly after I made the decision to step away from the school. As it turned out, I had begun helping people bring books and engaging learning experiences to life in powerful ways even before I considered creating StoryBuilders. I was helping maximize the message of Hugh's book.

That's the power of books—they change how people think. When you change how people think, you change how they act. And when you change how they act, you change the world.

> That's the power of books—they change how people think.

I've seen this happen close to home. StoryBuilders collaborated with entrepreneur and reality TV star Rodman Schley to create his poignant book *The Outlier Mindset*. After reading it, one of my sons, who has an entrepreneurial bent, shared with me that he felt affirmed and seen for the first time as "an outlier." It raised his confidence and lifted his belief level about what he could do with his life.

When I shared that story with Rodman, he was deeply moved to see the impact of his message in such a real way. When we came alongside Rodman to help bring his book to life, I never imagined that our work would create something that would help my own son. But once again, that's the power of books. You just never know where they will go.

THE BOOKSTARTER QUESTIONS

If you are thinking about writing a nonfiction book of any kind to share your message, there are five critical BookStarter Questions we ask at the beginning of any project. It doesn't matter if it is an author's first book or thirtieth; the neat thing is that these questions really are about getting clarity on the message. So whether you're writing a book, speaking from a stage, or honing in on your BrandStory, they can help you.

By answering these questions and understanding the concepts behind them, you can begin to lay the foundation for not just a good book but a great book.

1. THE STORYFOCUS QUESTION

If someone were to read your book and remember only one thing, what would you want that one thing to be?

This is often the first question I ask at the beginning of any book project because it helps reveal the core message that burns within you—the one that drives you to share it with the world. Think about it. After someone finishes the book, they'll probably forget most of what they read. That's normal. So what would you definitely *not* want them to forget?

There's something about the psychology behind this question that helps the essence of a message percolate to the surface. What's interesting is how often people have a ready answer when I ask it. It's as if they have been brewing on it for a while, just waiting for the invitation to share it. This question gives you permission to do so.

I have found that an author's ability to answer this question is directly proportional to how much clarity the author has about the message. When you have confusion at the outset, you seldom get the results you want. Not having immediate clarity does not mean you shouldn't write a book;

it just means you have some work to do to get the clarity you need.

A book about everything is a book about nothing.

The thing to realize is that a book about everything is a book about nothing. In fact, we already have a book about everything. It's called the Internet.

And no one casually sits down and starts browsing through it. They at least begin by searching for something they want—cat videos, car repair tricks, interior design help, or whatever. In a counterintuitive way, limiting the scope of your message gives it greater power and potential to resonate with the people who are already searching for what you are saying.

You have to be able to focus your message, which means cutting things that don't fit your StoryFocus. This StoryFocus becomes the touchstone for the entire book because as you work your way through a manuscript, you create what I call a "content wave." As you write the book, you will realize that certain content you thought would fit in a particular place ends up not fitting as neatly as you had hoped. You may realize it is good but does not align with the StoryFocus. Thus, it gets washed forward through the chapters or out of the book entirely—and that's okay.

2. THE NEEDLE MOVER QUESTION

How do you want the world to change as
a result of your book's impact?

This one is easy to overlook. A lot of authors get so excited about writing the book that they lose sight of why they want to write it in the first place. This may be one of the most important questions because it is the *why* that will sustain you when the going gets tough.

What impact do you want the book to have once you finish it? How do you want your StoryFocus to change the world? Get real as you think about this. Don't leave it as something vague such as "I want to help people." Make

When you move that needle you want to move, how will it make you feel?

it specific—"I want to change the way entrepreneurs think about customer service so their businesses interact with people differently every single day. And that will change how likely their business is to succeed and continue to serve others."

The key here is to not simply describe the impact but to connect emotionally with it. When you move that needle you want to move, how will it make you feel? Sit with that emotion and visualize what it will be like when someone tells you that your book changed how they do business and has made a difference for them and their team.

Go ahead and dream big here. Don't limit the possibilities. What is the potential impact you'd ideally like your book to have?

When you answer that question, you'll get clarity on the intended impact of your book. That will give you the means to measure your success in the future and the emotional fuel to propel you forward through the inevitable challenges.

3. THE IDEAL AUDIENCE QUESTION

Who is your audience, and what do they really want?

This question sounds a lot like the Attention question from the StoryTelling Structure we introduced in Chapter 2—and for good reason. It is. Just like your BrandStory, a book is *about* your ideas and message, but it ultimately is not *for* you. Many authors think only about what they want to say and not about what their intended audience wants or needs to hear. The effective ones focus on the latter.

I suggest working through the same three-circle exercise here as in the last chapter.

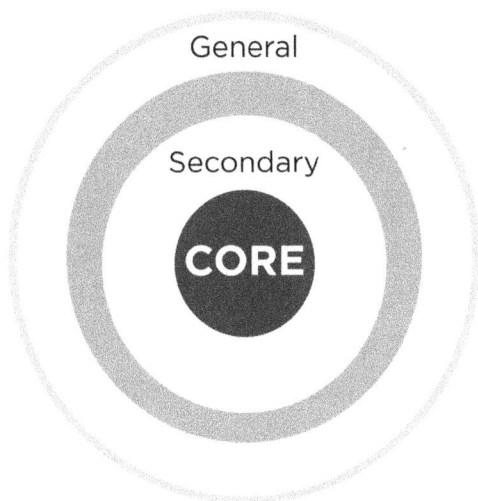

Circle 1: Who is your core audience? These are the people your book will help the most and will be most open to hearing it. Once again, these may closely resemble the person you once were. Perhaps ask yourself this version of the question: If your book resonated with no one but this group of people, who would that be? Answer with as much detail as possible to give yourself the clearest picture of the person you are writing this book for.

Circle 2: Who is your secondary audience? As you narrow down your focus to your core audience, you'll likely stumble across other groups that aren't quite at the center of it but do struggle with the same problems to some extent and would benefit from your message. Keep them in mind as you plan your book. Depending on your message, some of them may one day become your core audience, while others may influence people in your core audience to read your book. Don't ignore them, but don't fully focus your message on them.

Circle 3: Who is your general audience? Write the book for your core audience. Invite your secondary audience to join and potentially become part of your core audience if relevant. Only then should you give thought to how the rest of the world may interact with your message. If they like it, great, but they are not who you write for. Be aware of them, but don't let them determine your message focus.

Sometimes I speak with aspiring authors who tell me that their book is for "everyone." I mean, who wouldn't benefit from reading your book, right? Wrong. To repeat what I said earlier, a book for everyone is a book for no one. If you write a book intended for everyone, no one will think it is for them (because deep down, all of us think we're special).

A book for everyone is a book for no one.

Going back to your core audience, readers have to be able to see themselves as potential readers of your book, and the best way to do that is to create a reading experience that invites them specifically into the conversation. Think of it as a handwritten invitation with their name on it in calligraphy. That's how you want your core audience to feel as they pick up your book and begin to read.

After you determine the *who*, think about the *what*. Your book must resonate with what your core audience wants. So what do they want … really? This critical question shapes everything from the title of your book to the structure to the strategy to get the word out about it. People are not naturally interested in what you have to say. They are intrinsically motivated to seek what *they* want. What problems do they have that your book solves? How do they talk about those problems? How does your message help solve those problems? All these questions should shape the fundamental direction of the book before you ever write one word.

A common mistake authors often make is to choose a title for the book that appeals to them, the author. That could be something they think is clever, cute, or cool. The problem is that the reader doesn't care what you think—they only know what they want. When you know what they want, you are well on your way to finding a title that draws them in and promises a solution to the problem they have or the pain they feel.

Remember, it's not about you.

4. THE STORYSTRATEGY QUESTION

How will this book help you get where you want to go?

I know I've said this a lot—your book is not about you. That's true. And yet you do need to think about how the book fits into your big-picture plans for the future. **Begin your book with the end in mind.**

What is your vision for what you are building by sharing your message? Are you an entrepreneur looking to grow your business? Are you a business professional seeking great impact and possibly looking to establish your personal brand? Or are you a speaker, coach, consultant, or thought leader who wants to establish core intellectual property that you can leverage to help create a movement? To paraphrase Stephen Covey, you should begin your book with the end in mind.

Whatever it may be, once you think about the audience you want to reach, think about what you want the book to do. This exercise can be challenging for authors when they don't have clarity about what that bigger purpose might be other than to "help people." That's a noble aim, for sure, but a little thought can help you craft a deeper, more sustainable strategy that can actually position you to help more people.

For example, if you want to write a book about your unique perspective or plans to help end human trafficking, you may want to give some thought to how the book will support what you are doing to make that happen. Will you use profits to fund an organization you will build? Or do you just want to get the word out about the problem?

If you want to write a book that helps people with personal or leadership growth, you may want to create a business model that positions you to serve readers further through coaching, consulting, and learning experiences that build on the concept you share in your book. If you want to write a book about your unique approach to some aspect of business, you'll want to be strategic about how the book aligns with your overarching career strategy.

This exercise will also help shape how you choose the path to bring your book to life. If you just need a "business card" type of book, then you may be able to do it all on your own and self-publish. On the other hand, if you need a quality book to represent you and your brand well, you probably should collaborate with experts to make sure it does what you need it to do. The only thing worse than having no book is having one that does more harm than good. I'm sure we've all seen those books before. Don't be that author.

5. THE COFFEE SHOP QUESTION

*If I were struggling with the problem you solve
and we met up for coffee, what steps would
you take me through to help me solve it?*

This powerful question offers a casual way for you to get at the heart of *how* you do what you do. It was inspired by Jesse Barnett, one of our StoryDirectors at StoryBuilders, after he realized that some authors struggle to clearly see how they naturally do what they do. Even if you've spent a lot of time thinking about your message, it can still be challenging to distill it into actionable steps or an accessible structure when you're put on the spot (the dreaded Blank Page Syndrome). But most people already do what they want to write about; they just need to capture what they already do.

This question helps an author think through the Solution portion of the book. Ask yourself this: What is the actual process I give (or would give) people to work through in order to solve the problem I want them to solve? What do they need to know, say, or do differently to experience transformation?

And is there a particular order in which they should do those things?

Thinking about the Solution as a series of actions, principles, or processes forces an author to get more granular at the beginning of a project without getting lost in the weeds. Is it a seven-step process? Are there three phases of understanding? Are there key stages to the transformation? Are there certain habits your reader needs to practice to achieve the result they desire?

A good example would be this book itself. In Chapter 1, I introduced you to the Story EcoSystem™ and the three phases of growth: Message Maker (your BrandStory); Message Multiplier (your book); and your Message Monetizer (your IP). In doing so, I gave you a clear path to follow to maximize impact, influence, and income by telling your story. Then in Chapter 2, I shared the StoryTelling Structure you can leverage to bring each of those messaging tools to life. Now we are drilling deeper into each phase and applying the StoryTelling Structure and lessons from it to build your own Story EcoSystem™.

This question is also designed to begin to identify your own unique IP. We'll get into this more in the next chapter, but for now, the same principle we discussed in the BrandStory applies here too. Once you figure out the process or steps involved in whatever solution you offer, name it in a way that signals to your reader that it solves their problem (remember, it's not *for* you). In this book, for example, the solution of Your Story EcoSystem™ implies that it's (a) about *you*, (b) about your *story*, and (c) how to *grow* it.

Your solution may be unique to you, but that doesn't mean it shouldn't also feel familiar to the reader. And that's where it pays to have a proven structure around which you can build your book. So when you're ready, the next chapter will walk you through the final Book Starter Question to show you how to build a book structure your reader will love.

YOUR ADVANTAGE ACTIVITIES

If you don't know your *why* and *what*, your message won't be clear, your thoughts around that message will be convoluted, and your book will not speak to your audience the way you want it to.

So before you jump into writing your book or anything else, take some time to get clarity about your book message using the BookStarter Questions below.

1. **The StoryFocus Question:** If someone were to read your book and remember only one thing, what would you want that one thing to be?

2. **The Needle Mover Question:** How do you want the world to change as a result of your book's impact?

3. **The Ideal Audience Question:** Who is your audience, and what do they really want?

4. **The StoryStrategy Question:** How will this book help you get where you want to go?

5. **The Coffee Shop Question:** If I were struggling with the problem you solve and we met up for coffee, what steps would you take me through to help me solve it?

If you want more support to act on what you learn in this book, visit *YourStoryAdvantage.com/ FreeResources* or scan the QR code to discover FREE resources to help you maximize your story.

5

How to Structure
Your Book

Chris Winton grew up in the inner city of Memphis. A smart and active kid, he had straight A's until he reached high school. Then his grades started to slip as he worked two jobs to help support his family. Even still, Chris had big dreams. He wanted to be the CEO of a Fortune 500 company—*within ten years of graduating from high school*. But with no clear path forward and no time to study to raise his GPA, there was a good chance Chris's dream would remain just that.

One day during his senior year, Chris's guidance counselor encouraged him to attend a presentation by an organization called INROADS that taught leadership skills to high-achieving minority young people. Chris went to the meeting even though he knew he didn't have the minimum GPA required to join the group. However, he had the right attitude and work ethic—he'd already been promoted to supervisor at one of his jobs.

Going to that meeting changed his life. Chris's time at INROADS and his one-on-one meetings with Managing Director Alfonzo Alexander made his dream seem possible. INROADS helped him develop his leadership skills and excel in both school and work. Alfonzo taught him that a great leader is always reaching down with one hand to lift others up while using the other hand to continue reaching higher.

After high school, Chris graduated from the University of Memphis with a degree in Management Information Systems and started working for FedEx as a technician in the information technology (IT) department. Before long, he was already climbing the corporate ladder, earning promotion after promotion. Eventually he accepted a position with FedEx in Atlanta, Georgia, and relocated with his new wife. All was good—great, in fact. He bought a new house, drove nice cars, and dressed in expensive suits.

Then one morning, Chris found himself sitting in his car, clenching the leather-bound steering wheel, staring at the garage door, and thinking, *What had happened to my dream of becoming a CEO?* Ten years had passed, and he had completely forgotten his high school goal.

So he took the next logical step and earned his MBA. While the degree certainly helped, it didn't catapult him into the corner office like he thought it would.

But Chris had come to know leadership inside and out. In addition to his academic background, he had a natural talent for it *and* practical experience demonstrating his qualifications. But FedEx was a huge company, and it was sometimes hard to get noticed.

That's when Chris got the idea to write a book to amplify his story and clarify his leadership philosophy. Like most of our StoryPartners, Chris had a lot of ideas, but he needed something sticky, something memorable that distilled his message into a replicable process for readers. He wanted his book not only to mark him as an expert on leadership but also to help other people find their way forward. As Chris worked with us, we discussed the problem his ideal reader faced (how to grow leadership know-how) and helped clarify the four most important actions for any leader to take. Those actions became the basis for Chris's signature IP and the framework of his book.

Next, we determined which stories from Chris's life best illustrated the points he wanted to make. After putting all these pieces together, Chris's book, *C-4 Leadership: Ignite Your Career. Shatter Expectations. Take Charge of Your Life*, became the calling card he needed to move his career forward.

Soon after its publication, the book found its way into the hands of FedEx legend Fred Smith. He loved it, and soon

Chris was promoted to vice president of Human Resources. Chris has continued his explosive career at Tesla and Comcast while creating a speaking platform that has taken him all over the country.

Chris had the ideas. He had the experience. And he had the story. But what made his book as powerful and as successful as it has been was sharing it in an intentional way that really connected with his target audience. The right structure makes your impact easy.

DON'T WRITE JELL-O

Why is structure so important? In a word—bones. Without bones forming the structure of your body, you'd just be Jell-O on the floor. Without structure, your book is a jumble of words on the page. Don't write Jell-O.

But not any old structure will do. Recall The StoryMultiplier Formula™ from Chapter 1.

$$WHO \times S = I^3$$

Your impact, influence, and income all depend on the S—how well you tell your *story*. Structure can make or break your book. Using the wrong structure, a bad structure, or no structure at all is like multiplying by zero (for those nonmath majors like me, that means you always get nothing but zero).

That brings us to the sixth Book Starter Question.

6. THE STORYSTRUCTURE QUESTION

How will you structure your book for the best possible reader experience?

Every author knows you can't just throw words on a page and hope they randomly turn into a great book (although some have tried). However, most authors struggle with how to organize their thoughts into a structure that makes sense for the reader.

Every good book has a flow to it, an intentional structure that guides the reader's experience. Remember in Chapter 2 how I talked about the power of Disney's story structure? It's the same with nonfiction books. When a book doesn't have that cohesive flow to it, the message feels disjointed. The reader feels disconnected and therefore will be unlikely to finish reading.

In order to serve your core audience well, the structure of your book needs to make sense to *them* as you guide them from what they know now to what they need to know to get what they really want.

The structure is a guideline, not a rigid framework.

Once again, I turn to The StoryTelling Structure™ as a guide for creating a great book experience. Because it follows the natural proven flow of storytelling, it points us to what readers expect to experience in the flow of any story. However, keep in mind that the structure is a guideline, not a rigid framework. The structure helps create a plan and get started, but the science frees you as an author to create your art within those guidelines.

It's true that there are many successful books that don't seem to follow this structure, at least not on the surface. But all of them have taken the elements of The StoryTelling Structure™ into account in some way to create a great reader experience. Most good books do follow this flow, even if you can't always identify each section of the structure explicitly. So I suggest using this structure as a starting point to plan your book. You can deviate from it, of course, but you need to know why you intentionally want to do so.

Think of the structure shaping your book in two ways: The entire book has a structure and flow, *and* each chapter within the book has a structure and flow. We'll address both here.

THE OPENING CHAPTERS: THE FOUNDATION

Your Opening Chapter: Attention

The StoryTelling Structure™ begins with Step One: Attention. So Chapter 1 of your book is all about capturing and holding the reader's attention. It's in the first few chapters that a reader will decide whether or not to keep reading. The fact that they started doesn't mean they will finish.

When we write a great book at StoryBuilders, we go even deeper and use The StoryTelling Structure™ to map out the first chapter in a way that makes readers feel comfortable or "just right." (Remember The Connection Continuum?)

Keep in mind that in most instances, you need to introduce yourself to the reader, never assuming the person who picked up the book already knows who you are and why they should listen to you. However, you want to share your story strategically—only the parts that will help the reader connect with you so they'll listen to what you have to say.

When crafted intentionally, Chapter 1 does several things:

- **Attention:** Pulls the reader in and captures their interest. This can happen with an engaging story, a startling statistic, a captivating question, a shocking statement, or other techniques. For example, the first chapter of this book began with the story of how I got here. Additionally, every subsequent chapter has started with a story that illustrates the main message of the content.

- **Tension:** Identifies the problem readers struggle with in a way that has them nodding along as they read. You want them thinking you are reading their mental mail, so it is worth the time to invest in getting the words just right. The main tension of the book is laid out in Chapter 1 as the Story Traps that I'm teaching you how to overcome.

- **Connection:** Emotionally connects the reader to the author and establishes the author as a trusted voice of authority on the subject. You want to demonstrate that you have felt the reader's pain and had success in resolving it. My initial connection was telling you the story of my journey of starting StoryBuilders, but now I'm showing you how to build your Story EcoSystem™ and write a book—demonstrating my credentials as a writer and publisher throughout.

- **Solution:** Casts a vision for the big-picture solution that lies on the pages to come so the reader knows where you want to take them. No one wants to read a book without some awareness of what lies ahead. Establishing clear expectations gives the reader confidence to keep turning the page. For example, the

Solution to the problem of not having the influence, impact, and income you want is to build your Story EcoSystem™ with your BrandStory, your book, and your IP.

- **Action:** Invites readers to continue reading and take the actions needed to solve their problems. Make this intentional with a call to "join me" in some way and reference the promise you make to them if they keep reading. You can also consider, depending on the nature of the book, if you want them to begin reflecting, processing, or engaging in any activities. In this book, there are activities at the end of every chapter to help you get started on each solution and links to get even more resources to help you on your journey. (And there will be some cool opportunities at the end of the book too.)

Chapter 2: Tension

Chapter 2 focuses on Step Two: Tension. The aim of this chapter is to amplify the pain the reader feels. The reality is that we often find ways to numb ourselves to the pain of our challenges so we can minimize or ignore them to get by. But we'll never be motivated to solve a problem that doesn't hurt us enough to change.

> **We all tend to run from tension in our lives, but mountains make the best settings for the most memorable stories.**

We all tend to run from tension in our lives, but mountains make the best settings for the most memorable stories. So don't gloss over the problems or mountains the reader faces. Amplify them instead. Give them the gift of a cold splash of reality to help them see the need for change.

By the end of Chapter 2, you want the reader to decide that if they do nothing else, they must finish the rest of your book to find the solution to their problem. Unfortunately, a lot of readers give up on books after Chapter 2, partly because they're not convinced they have a problem worth solving. It's your job as the author to keep them turning the pages.

Chapter 3: Connection

For Chapter 3, I suggest focusing on Step Three: Connection and setting up the reader for Step Four: Solution. This is an opportunity to go deeper with your own story, thus deepening your connection with the readers. Here especially, it may be helpful to share how you wrestled with the same challenges they face and how you overcame them.

Under our structure, this chapter gives you the greatest flexibility for framing your book. We've worked on many books that follow this format closely, but some have expanded to two chapters where critical nuances of the message needed to be explained before diving into the rest of the book.

Other times it expanded into an entire section with multiple chapters when we felt the need to establish a stronger foundation for the reader or when we knew the reader would need to solve one key problem before being open to receive the solution.

This chapter should set up the Solution section to follow.

THE SOLUTION CHAPTERS: THE TOOLS TO SUCCEED

After you've grabbed the readers' attention and given them a preview of what to expect and how you can help them, it's time to lay out that solution in a clear and easy-to-follow manner. This is the meat of the book, the heart of the IP you can develop later in the next phase of your Story EcoSystem™.

Depending on how you solve the problem your book is about, each chapter may be a stand-alone solution in and of itself. Or each chapter could be one part of a multi-step solution—steps that must be completed in a particular sequence to achieve the desired results. Regardless, you can write each of them following the same structure.

Chapter 4 and Beyond: Solution

Chapters 4 and beyond focus on Step Four: Solution. This is your core content, the heart of what your book is about. Think of it as the success path, your proven process, and all the guidance of how to do it and apply it.

This core content can have any number of chapters, but it should usually be anywhere from three to seven. (People generally get overwhelmed by more than seven chapters in a given section.) Your core content could be longer if broken up into smaller sections or parts, but it all depends on the unique content of the book. You always want the reader to feel that the process is manageable.

Keep it simple. (This may be more difficult than you think when you are the subject matter expert.) You could go deep on your message; however, as the old adage goes, if no one is following you, you're not leading anyone anywhere; you're just taking a walk by yourself. It might be enjoyable for you but not helpful to others.

StoryBuilders creates all our chapters using The Storytelling Structure™, but we go a layer deeper in this Solution section of the book. Here we actually add another step in the process—call it Step 4.5—to give it the depth it needs: Application.

Here's how it works when framing a Solution section chapter.

Attention: Often a story serves to grab attention and illustrate the Main Message of the chapter. In this chapter, for example, the story of Glenn Cunningham illustrated the main message—*a book can go places you will never go and touch more people than you will ever know.*

Tension: How much space is needed to amplify or clarify the problem being solved *in that core chapter* will vary. It could require several paragraphs, an entire subsection, or as little as a passing mention. Hold the structure loosely.

Connection: Keep holding the structure loosely as well since you have already established your story earlier in the book. This may be an opportunity to share more personal stories if they illustrate and support the main message of the chapter. If not, don't feel like you must force your story in. Perhaps a passing mention of your experience may be all that is needed. Look for the connection, but don't try to force it.

Solution: We like to distill this into a single Solution Statement, a clear and sticky expression of what the reader needs to do to take the action you propose in the chapter. If Chapter 1 is the 30,000-foot view of the problem, think of this as the 15,000-foot view. You are much closer to landing the plane but still need to convince readers that they should.

Application: This is a new section of the structure for use only in Solution chapters. It is all about landing the plane. It's the how-to, the nuts and bolts, and the gritty details about how to actually get this done. Here is where you might share deeper IP, tips and

tricks, or concrete behaviors the reader can develop to apply the solution statement.

What you are reading right now is, in fact, an example of the Application section of this chapter. We're going deeper to explain in more detail how to actually structure your book at a practical level. We may even be going too deep for some readers who just want someone to help them write their book (more on that later). This Application section will typically take up most of the chapter in this section of your book.

Action: The final section of a Solution chapter can vary depending on your answer to the StoryStrategy Question: What is the end that you have in mind?

How active do you want the reader to be? Do you want them to:

- Just read as you invite them to act?

- Jump-start their actions with reflection questions or activities?

- Go elsewhere (your website or other locations) to discover, learn, or do more?

Your overarching strategy will help shape how you wrap up each chapter, depending on what action you want the reader to take next. In this chapter you are reading now, for example, we offer the option to take action right away with activities, *and* we invite you to get even more tools, resources, and support to bring your book to life.

We use two questions to help decide this.

1. How deep do you want the reader to reflect?

2. How complex is the action you want them to take?

To best decide how to approach this section, I suggest using our Reader Action Matrix to choose the approach that works for you and your reader.

THE **Reader Action Matrix**

R E F L E C T I O N	**D E E P**	**Guided**	**Focused**
	L I G H T	**Prescriptive**	**Suggestive**
		SIGNIFICANT	SIMPLE

ACTION

1. **Guided:** Deep Reflection / Complex Action
2. **Focused:** Deep Reflection / Simple Action
3. **Prescriptive:** Light Reflection / Complex Action
4. **Suggestive:** Light Reflection / Simple Action

REFLECTION	ACTION
Deep Reflection: • Assessments • Journaling • Asking probing "push-stop" questions • Gathering input • Introspection	**Complex Action:** • Activities designed to produce transformation • Change how the reader does something • Connect with you for guidance • Take outside-the-book action (scan, click, etc.)
Light Reflection: • Questions based on the reading • Start the reader thinking process • Ask casual "push-pause" questions	**Simple Action:** • Next-best steps • Try this … or that • What if you …?

Give the reader psychological closure in each chapter.

You can mix and match these approaches, depending on the flow of the book. There is no hard and fast rule here. Just be consistent to make sure the reader knows what to expect. In other words, don't shift from the Suggestive mode in one chapter to the Guided mode and then back again. It will leave readers feeling disoriented.

Another trick to use in the Action section of any chapter is to give the reader psychological closure in each chapter. For example, in Chapter 4, I began with the inspiring story of Glenn Cunningham's incredible persistence and how his refusal to quit led to his success as a runner. To help close the loop for readers, I might have chosen to circle back to that story by sharing a little more to drive home its power. For instance, I might have said this:

> Glenn's refusal to quit would be an amazing inspirational story if it only ended there. But Glenn kept running. He leveraged his fame as a runner to open a ranch for kids from troubled backgrounds.
>
> Over the next thirty years, Glenn and his wife hosted more than 10,000 children whose lives were transformed—all because that seven-year-old boy refused to quit in the face of unthinkable adversity. The same kind of impact is available to all who live a story worth telling and share it well.

As a final touch, I always love adding a little tease to set up what comes next for the reader. It need not be as direct as "in the next chapter, I'll tell you …." It could be as subtle as "once you see how a book can multiply your message, you can turn to the question so many authors and aspiring thought leaders have asked: How do I leverage it to make more money?" The point is to let the reader know where they are in the overarching plan you shared in Chapter 1. A disoriented reader won't remain a reader for long.

THE CONCLUSION: ACTION TO TAKE

Finally, there should be a Conclusion to the entire book. It might be one final chapter or a couple shorter chapters. Again, it all depends on what you're presenting to the reader.

However, the focus of the Conclusion is Step Five: Action. Don't just come to a sudden stop after you share your Solution content and then kick the reader out. Give the same sense of psychological closure for the entire book as you do in each chapter, and consider what you want the reader to do next.

It may be an inspirational call to believe something, an invitation to join your community, or a way to connect further and go deeper. There are plenty of options. Whatever you choose, give readers a clear call to action. Remember, you are the expert, so what do you think they should do next?

Remember to think of The StoryTelling Structure™ as your guideline. When you start with this framework, you are guaranteed to be in a much better place than hurling chapters against the wall and hoping they stick. When you deviate from it, you simply need to be able to explain why it makes sense to do so.

At StoryBuilders, we go deeper on this book-creation process all day, every day when working directly with authors as part of our StoryStrategy Service. Whether you choose to become one of these authors or not, these BookStarter Questions will help you create momentum. Then before you know it, your book will begin to come to life.

And of course, once you see how a book can multiply your message when you structure it well to maximize your impact, you can turn to the question so many authors and aspiring thought leaders have asked: *How do I leverage it to make more money?*

YOUR ADVANTAGE ACTIVITIES

Now it's time to pull all your thoughts together from the last two chapters into a rough sketch of the framework for your book.

Use the rough framework below to start jotting down your thoughts on how to answer the **StoryStructure Question:** How will you structure your book for the best possible reader experience?

The Foundation
Chapter 1: Attention

Chapter 2: Tension

Chapter 3: Connection

The Solution
Chapter 4

Chapter 5

Chapter 6

Chapter 7

Chapter 8

Chapter 9

The Conclusion
Chapter 10

If you want more support to act on what you learn in this book, visit *YourStoryAdvantage.com/ FreeResources* or scan the QR code to discover FREE resources to help you maximize your story.

6

The Message Monetizer: Your IP

He was a C student at best. The truth was, no one expected much from him. His home life was humble. At one point, his single mom worked three jobs making about ninety dollars a week just to keep a trailer-park roof over their heads. Due to his poor grades and struggles with dyslexia, he didn't go to college. But no matter what other people might have thought of him, he always knew he was meant for something more.

He worked hard and eventually became the owner of an automobile collision-repair shop, a car dealership, and some apartment buildings. But still, he was always grinding to make ends meet. He knew there had to be a better way to earn a living.

Then he happened to watch an infomercial featuring inspirational guru Tony Robbins. (Remember those? "But wait—there's more! Call this toll-free number. Operators are standing by!") Tony had something he didn't—knowledge. So, he picked up the phone and gave the salesperson his credit card information. A few weeks later, he was deep-diving into Tony's Personal Power course. As soon as he listened to the first lesson, he knew he hadn't bought a product; he had bought an opportunity.

Looking back now, he realizes that the number-one thing he took away from that experience was the concept of paying someone for their expertise. That knowledge changed him in fundamental ways. In fact, the idea excited him so much that he wanted to share his experience to help other people go farther, faster.

With no support from his family and no idea how to film an infomercial, hold product in a warehouse, or buy TV airtime, he created a course that shared his knowledge of buying and selling cars. And then he made his first sale. He had actual proof that he could sell his story and expertise.

He then created a course on how to sell real estate, and it became the world's number-one knowledge product on real estate. But Dean Graziosi was just getting started.

Almost three decades later, Dean's training courses have created massive passive income, and his brands have generated over a billion dollars in sales. He also now calls Tony Robbins his business partner and friend.

Because of their pioneering efforts to move the knowledge economy forward, Dean and Tony have been able to do a lot of good in the world, not only empowering countless people to monetize their messages but also hosting other high-impact work—providing millions of meals through Feeding America, donating funds to help free kids from slavery, building schools in other countries, and helping the Phoenix Children's Hospital create a vibrant, welcoming area with toys, colorful walls, and TVs to help kids feel more at ease during their visits.

Unsurprisingly, Dean's breakthrough began when he started with his story. But his story reveals a deeper truth. When people value your message, you make more money doing what you love to do.

WHAT MONEY REALLY REPRESENTS

Most of us have no problem with the idea of making more money. However, I've found a significant number of people do, in fact, have an aversion to monetizing their Meaningful Message. Perhaps they see a disconnect between helping people and making money. This disconnect could come from childhood or family experiences or have been shaped by societal, religious, or philosophical views about serving others.

I get it. I grew up in a wonderful family and church environment that strongly emphasized serving others. But I found that emphasis on service could often become an unintentional call to be a doormat for others—for free. As a result, I struggle at times to monetize my message, even if it's specific knowledge I've worked hard to learn and develop. The script that plays in my head is that if I really care about people, I should give it away for free. I've since come to realize that thinking is incorrect.

Money is a placeholder for value. If our Meaningful Message actually delivers value to people, then it only makes sense that those people who are willing and able will give you money to access it, use it, and solve problems with it.

That doesn't mean money is the only value that will come your way. You may make connections and relationships or experience deep fulfillment in hearing the stories of lives transformed by what you shared and how you shared it. Yet the most convenient way for someone to convey value to you is by giving you money. Don't be afraid to accept it and even expect it.

Money is a convenient and countable measure of your impact and influence. If you deliver value to the world, the world will deliver value to you.

> **If you deliver value to the world, the world will deliver value to you.**

After all, if your knowledge was a physical product like a car, a cell phone, or a cupcake, would you have the same hesitation about putting a price on it? You spent time and resources getting all the pieces you needed to put together that car, phone, or cupcake. Would you give it away for free all the time? Or would you want to share it *and* receive the resources you need to keep making it and sharing it over and over again with others?

Let's return to the Story Multiplier Formula™ from Chapter 1.

$$WHO \times S = I^3$$

Who you are, multiplied by how well you tell **your Story**, equals I cubed—**Impact, Influence,** and **Income.** These three I's are interconnected—when one increases, the other two are likely to increase as well. When all three increase, your results are often multiplied exponentially.

Aversion to making money from your message is not the only challenge people encounter. When considering monetizing their message, the same common traps that we encountered in Chapter 1 also apply here.

1. **The Confidence Trap: You diminish it.** The thought of someone paying you money to experience your Meaningful Message does require a level of self-confidence. Only you can choose to embrace it. Don't deify others and diminish yourself. You've worked hard for the knowledge you have, and there's someone in the world right now who would pay you for that expertise. You have value, and you bring value, so allow others to give value back to you.

2. **The Chaos Trap: You paralyze it.** It's easy to get caught in the Creativity Conundrum at this stage of your storytelling. There is no shortage of ideas about how to monetize your story. The more people you talk to, the more opinions you'll encounter about the best way to do it. The best advice I have here is to do your homework and learn all you can about all your viable options, but don't get caught up at this research stage. At the end of the day, I suggest two things: Identify your lowest hanging fruit (the easiest path to success for you), and choose the path that feels most comfortable to you.

> Identify your lowest hanging fruit and choose the path that feels most comfortable to you.

Think about what types of services you deliver and focus on what you do well. Rather than spreading yourself too thin trying to chase all your ideas at once and getting nowhere despite all the work, pick one and focus on it while you learn and develop one or two more.

3. **The Normalcy Trap: You undervalue it.** Getting out of this trap often requires enlisting help from others who have a more objective view of the value you deliver to the world. It's easy for you to undervalue the impact of your message because it feels normal to you. You may think, *Who would pay for this?* And so you get caught up giving away everything and becoming a doormat to a certain extent. Yet when you invite other respected

voices to give you a candid assessment of your message potential, you may open doors you never realized were available to you and help a lot more people along the way.

4. **The Hidden Cost Trap: You waste it.** The Story EcoSystem™ builds as it grows, naturally expanding with each step, moving from your Meaningful Message and BrandStory to your core content in a book, and then to a plethora of ways to monetize your intellectual property. Everyone who writes a book should give some serious thought—*as they write the book*—to how they can monetize their message beyond the book. That requires some thought effort, but it takes full advantage of the multiplier effect of a book by positioning you with additional pathways to monetize your message.

5. **The Knowledge Trap: You don't know what to do with it.** This may be the biggest trap people fall into at this phase of the Story EcoSystem™ as there are many possible pathways. It seems as if there's a lot to learn, which is true, but think about it. Your entire life has been spent learning to do something new. At one point, you couldn't talk. At one point, you couldn't walk. At one point, you couldn't read. At one point, you had not developed the unique talents and skills that are now a natural part of who you are. You can learn all you need to learn to steward your story well in this phase of your growth without becoming an expert on everything. You

can find other people who *are* experts and lean into them to monetize your message.

YOUR IP MONETIZER THOUGHT STARTER

You may be thinking, *Okay, Bill, I get it. I could do a lot of cool stuff with my message and possibly make more money, but what kind of stuff exactly?*

The reality is that how you might make money from monetizing your message is bound only by your imagination, changing technology, and your willingness to grow. Here are a few ideas of how you could monetize your message, and all of them work especially well as a follow-up to your book.

- **Memberships.** People pay you on a regular basis for access to your knowledge and your message. Think of it as a subscription service.

- **Workshops.** These in-person events are popular ways to bring together groups of people, often within the same organization, to grow and learn together. They can be half-day, full-day, or multiple-day events.

- **Licensing.** This is a way to expand the workshop experience. You could license other people to use your intellectual property in their own settings, such as within larger organizations or in their specific fields. For example, a business consultant may want to use the ideas you have packaged in their own consulting efforts, and they would pay you for the privilege to do so.

- **Coaching Programs.** These programs can be either one-to-one or one-to-many group coaching efforts that give you direct access to people you or your team can coach to greater success. We've created coaching programs ranging anywhere from a single year program to several-year programs. The time required for coaching depends on the nature of the need.

- **Live and Virtual Events.** Nothing beats getting in the room with people and hosting your own conference, seminar, or gathering of some sort that people pay to attend—except now it doesn't have to be in person thanks to the Internet. You can leverage technology to host virtual events as well. Just know that there are pros and cons to each approach. You don't have to be an expert in either one to do these well. You just need to find and partner with people who have that expertise.

- **Masterminds.** As you climb the success ladder, you may find that people are willing to pay you for access to your wisdom, insights, and methods. In addition, if you gather a group of like-minded people around you, the synergy from each member adds even greater value to the group. As a result, they will be willing and able to pay you to be part of such a group as a digital masterclass.

- **Digital Masterclass.** We call these digital learning experiences. They can take the form of a masterclass or an online course of some sort. The beauty of these learning experiences is that you can create the content once, often capturing core teaching via video animation and a variety of instructional experiences, and then sell it many times to most effectively leverage your investment of time and money. The easiest way to monetize your book message is by partnering with a team like StoryBuilders that can deliver not only a compelling book but also an engaging learning experience. People will gladly pay more money, at least ten times as much as for a book, to access a deeper application of your Meaningful Message.

- **Keynotes and Speeches.** This is a classic example of how to monetize your message and probably the one you're most familiar with—you get paid to speak to an audience about your story. It's a pretty straightforward approach, and there are a lot of experts who can coach you on how to do that well. One thing to consider is whether you want to get paid a fee to speak or if you want the opportunity to sell your services or product at the event. From the stage, we partner with a number of people who've had considerable success doing one or the other, but usually not both as a primary focus.

- **Digital Products.** These offerings are typically standalone. Unlike a digital masterclass, these offerings are typically simpler tools, frameworks, or single learning sessions that are micro-focused on a particular need instead of a comprehensive solution to a larger problem. You can find some examples of these types of products at mystorybuilders.com.

- **Physical Products.** Once again, there's no shortage of things to sell in this world. When most people think of a product, they think of something they can touch or put to use in a physical space. If that's the business you are in, then you certainly should lean into it and consider supplementing it with nonphysical or digital offerings. However, if you're naturally in the idea (nonphysical offering) space, you may want to expand your thinking to include possible physical products such as a journal brand, a swag, or a branded clothing line. You don't have to commit to it right now. Just think about it and let the ideas come to you.

Clearly, there are a lot of options, and this is only intended to get you started. I suggest scheduling blue-sky time when you can let the ideas flow, get them all out, and then sort through them later. Just remember that at the end of the day, your wisest move is to *pick one*. Focus on doing that well while you develop one or two others for the future.

THERE'S MORE THAN ONE WAY

Sometimes we just don't know what might be possible until we dare to ask, "What if?" I saw this happen when we had the privilege of creating The Secrets of Closing the Sale Masterclass. To bring this experience to life, we partnered with Kevin Harrington, the original shark from the hit TV show *Shark Tank*, and the Zig Ziglar family. Zig exemplified what it meant to have a Meaningful Message and share it via public speaking workshops and similar training experiences.

He also pioneered the use of technology to multiply his message in conjunction with his bestselling books such as *See You at the Top* and *Zig Ziglar's Secrets of Closing the Sale*. When these books came out, Zig leveraged audio cassette technology and then later video technology to monetize his message further (this was pre-2000s).

Unfortunately, Zig passed away in 2012. When we partnered with Kevin and the Ziglar family to bring the course to life in 2016, there was obviously no way for Zig to make a live appearance. Our options were limited—or so we thought. Initially, Kevin was going to talk about Zig's teaching, and we were going to use animated videos to bring

Zig's core stories and concepts to life. Then Kevin could add his own experiences, lessons, and insights to the mix to create a powerful experience. That might have been a winning formula … until something unexpected happened.

Someone found entire pallets of video recordings that Zig had made for a private client many years before and had never released to the public. What a treasure trove of video content! The only downside was that the video had been recorded in the classic 4:3 screen ratio, whereas most screens today use the 16:9 wide-screen format. So we put our heads together and came up with a creative way for both Zig and Kevin to share the screen.

We had Kevin standing in a studio, and next to him was a classic television, the massive kind you may have seen in your grandparents' house back in the day. After Kevin introduced the topic, he simply turned to the television, and thanks to the creative work of the video team, Zig came to life on the screen to share his incredibly engaging stories. When Zig's videos finished, Kevin returned to drive a point home or add his own insights and applications to today's sales environment.

Then we added animated shorts and some of Kevin's own content to the mix, mining his sales experiences to spotlight his unique secrets for selling. To top it all off, we created an interview format that played to Kevin's strengths of sharing stories on the spot in front of a camera.

We packaged all of it around the metaphor of secrets. Thus, the course was built around seven secret vaults that the participant would unlock as they made their way through the experience. It was a masterclass extraordinaire. It launched with sales over a million dollars and led to an updated edition of *Zig Ziglar's Secrets of Closing the Sale*, with new chapters added by Kevin Harrington.

That's just one example of the creativity that can be deployed to monetize a message. We've worked with countless others to do the same, like businessman Scott Grates and incredibly talented, popular speakers like John Foley—a former lead solo pilot for the Blue Angels and one of the most in-demand keynote speakers today. We partnered with John to clarify his BrandStory and create both his digital home site and engaging learning experiences to monetize his message. (As of this writing, we're also working on a new, compelling book.)

Another person we've come alongside is Molly Fletcher, one of the first top female sports agents who has since become a popular keynote speaker. We collaborated on a digital learning experience with her, helped structure her #1 *USA Today* bestselling book, and created virtual events in which her incredible team could share her messages with a wide variety of businesses.

It might seem like a single person with a specific message has an advantage in creating engaging intellectual property, but we also work with organizations all the time to do the same thing. One of our most rewarding experiences came from walking alongside a larger company called Neighborly.

It serves as a parent company for more than twenty service franchises. You may have seen many of them where you live—Mr. Appliance, Mr. Electric, Mr. Rooter, Molly Maid, Lawn Pride, Mosquito Joe, and others.

They wanted to develop the leaders they needed in order to grow. We helped them refine their existing messages and reimagine the curriculum they used to guide their leadership growth plans. Then we created a year-long program that combined in-person gatherings with online learning that could be replicated throughout their service companies to develop leaders. As a result, their entire family of companies is positioned to make more money and multiply its impact and influence.

Whatever your situation, organization, or cause, there are many ways for you to monetize your message. You just have to be willing to figure out how.

DISCOVER YOUR UNIQUE IP

If you've already done the work from the previous chapter, you have a head start on creating your unique intellectual property. Of course, you may already have some idea of the various components of your message. You may already have had considerable success sharing some of it with the world, or you may be at the beginning trying to figure out what to do with what's in your head.

No matter where you find yourself, the following three-step process will help you get clarity about your IP direction.

I call it the IP ID Tool because it helps you identify your intellectual property.

First, a word of caution. This process gets messy on purpose before it gets organized. Remember that it's the "simplicity on the other side of complexity" that we want. The only way to bring order to the idea clutter inside your head is to engage the messiness of it in order to reach that simplicity on the other side. The only way out is through.

THE IP ID TOOL: HOW TO IDENTIFY YOUR INTELLECTUAL PROPERTY

Step 1. SEARCH: Engage with Questions

- **What already exists?** Dump out all your existing content, whether from articles or books you've written, podcasts you've hosted or been a guest on, speeches you've delivered, courses you've offered, coaching plans you've created, you name it. Whatever it is, gather it all and lay them out on the table either physically or virtually. Don't worry about making it neat. Just get it out, all in one place.

- **What exists only in your head?** Next, jot down the unique methods or messages you use on a regular basis that don't already exist somewhere else. If it's helpful, you can use these five prompts to remind yourself what they are. What is often …

- Repeated?

- Recalled?

- Rewarding?

- Recognizable?

- Rhythmic?

- **What have other people said they value from you?**
Think back on all the times that someone has said, "I
really appreciate that you [fill in the blank]." Where
have people said they most value hearing from you
and on what topics? In what setting? What problems
were you solving for them?

Step 2. SORT: Discover the Patterns

What you're looking for in this step are what I call content
clusters—similar topics or themes that seem to bunch
together easily and naturally.

I must confess that I thoroughly enjoy this part of the
process because I'm naturally able to take in vast amounts of
information all at once and hold it all suspended in midair, as
it were, while I find the connections among them all.

The good news is that you don't have to have that strength
if it doesn't come naturally to you. We're happy to come
alongside you at this stage and help you discover the patterns
and processes. We have intentionally cultivated this specific
strength at StoryBuilders, but you can still follow the process

outlined below and be creative without it. Just find as many connections as possible.

- **What patterns and processes do you see?** Look for trends, topics, steps, systems—anything that naturally connects with other related items. Have fun sketching a mind map, bubble, or spider diagram on a sheet of paper.

- **Where do you see content clusters?** Identify where you see content easily and naturally coming together based on common themes or uses. What are those topics? Don't judge or evaluate them for now; just look for connections.

- **What does your audience want?** Keep your potential audience or customers in mind. Don't let them control your IP development. Just jot down pain points, needs, or desires they have, and look for ways your content clusters might connect and provide solutions for those pain points, needs, or desires.

Step 3. STRUCTURE: Build Your IP Framework

Now that you're beginning to see some order emerge from the creative chaos, it's time to release your inner organizer and build at least a loose framework you can clarify over time.

- **How might you organize your IP?** Look for steps to success, pieces in a process, categories of growth—anything that feels like a natural working framework.

Don't be concerned about whether everything fits into this new organization. In fact, you may come up with several possibilities of ways to organize your intellectual property, and that's okay. Generate as many as you can. You can test all of them later.

- **What overarching metaphor might you use?** Think about The Secrets of Closing the Sale Masterclass example I shared earlier. When we realized that the goal of the content was to reveal secrets, we expanded on the metaphor of sales vaults that the learner could open as they made their way through the digital experience. Thus, this secret vault metaphor shaped how we labeled each lesson, how we presented support materials, and even the imagery and design for the entire experience.

Think about imagery, storytelling, or examples that might bring your IP framework to life. Here are some ideas to get you started.

- Analogies: "It's like ..."
- Illustrations
- Mental pictures
- Examples
- Common themes
- Fun comparisons
- Shared imagery

- **What will you call your new IP structure?**
  Remember Seth Godin's advice that naming
  something permits us to store it, work on it, and talk
  to other people about it. Remember that naming your
  structure gives people the gift of clarity, even if you
  don't think it is all that unique.

No doubt you are already familiar with many simple
and popular IP structures, like Stephen Covey's *The
7 Habits of Highly Effective People,* John C. Maxwell's
The 5 Levels of Leadership, or Patrick Lencioni's *The
Five Dysfunctions of a Team.* Your title doesn't have to
have a number in it, but it should give the reader some
idea of what to expect from your IP.

In many ways, this Monetizing Your Message phase of the
Story EcoSystem™ is the most fun. You can do many unique
things to share your message with the world and multiply
your impact, influence, and income as a result of mastering
this concept.

The best part is that it never ends. You can always
reimagine, create new ideas, and find fresh messages and
methods to keep engaging your audience in ways that enrich
you as well.

YOUR ADVANTAGE ACTIVITY

If you haven't already done the work I've laid out in this chapter, I encourage you to push pause and do so.

If you prefer a downloadable or digital resource to make the process even easier, go to *YourStoryAdvantage.com/FreeResources* and download it for free.

Just promise me you'll actually put it to use.

Meet me at the beginning of Chapter 7 when you're done. I have one last secret to share with you.

If you want more support to act on what you learn in this book, visit *YourStoryAdvantage.com/FreeResources* or scan the QR code to discover FREE resources to help you maximize your story.

7

Go Farther Faster

I first met Greg Cagle while developing training and workshop experiences with John C. Maxwell and Maxwell Leadership. Greg was and continues to be one of the best live workshop facilitators I have ever met. He is also a top executive coach and business consultant in a class all his own.

At that time, he had a lot of valuable messages that could help a lot of business leaders multiply their impact, influence, and income, but in some ways, he felt stuck. He was blessed to be great at what he does. As a result, he was in high demand, so he struggled to find the time to turn his own ideas into products he could sell and still be proud of the outcome. He wanted to be sure that whatever he did represented his own commitment to excellence and quality, while also expressing his unique brand voice.

That's when we partnered with him. We began by developing his Story EcoSystem™. We helped him get clarity on his BrandStory, direction, and core message, and helped him through the work with his then-existing time constraints. Next, we collaborated with him to create his first book, *Be Weird: Succeed in Life and Business Simply by Being You.* That book serves as a manifesto of sorts for each person to embrace their own uniqueness, but to do so in a way that best invites constructive connection with the rest of the world. We then developed multiple workshops and training forums with him that have been used with some of the largest companies in the world, touching millions of lives. We did this all while Greg positioned himself for the next stage of his career, which has given him more time to do the things he wants to do now— spend more time with his family, continue to help develop the next group of leaders, and teach companies how to work better.

As often happens, though, Greg had more than one book inside of him. So we partnered again to write *The 4 Dimensions of Culture: And the Leaders Who Shape Them,* which epitomizes what is possible when someone intentionally develops their Story EcoSystem™. Greg came into the project with incredible ideas that he had honed over his years of coaching and consulting. We came into the project with our own fresh perspectives that helped elevate his message and create the unique intellectual property—the four dimensions that formed the framework of the book. We also developed a unique visual representation of those four dimensions to help simplify a complex topic.

But we weren't done yet.

Because Greg had seen the power of monetizing intellectual property, we collaborated on additional workshop experiences that opened the door for people to apply the insights from the book to their own businesses, teams, and organizations. We even took a unique approach in crafting those experiences and immersing participants in real-time creative scenarios that helped them apply what they had learned.

Greg was on a roll, but he wanted to find a way to touch more people to make a greater impact with his message, and he knew he couldn't achieve his goals on his own.

So once again, we collaborated to create a digital learning experience that would allow people to learn from Greg when he wasn't physically in the room. We fired up the creativity machine and came up with an innovative approach that combined multiple engaging mediums, unique activities, and Greg's own authentic style with high-quality video production. We shot on location at a historic building that gave the entire experience additional flair.

If you want to elevate, you must collaborate.

The journey with Greg has been a fun one to be sure, but also one that has resulted in a friendship, as often happens when we work with our StoryPartners. Greg understood the power of bringing in other people to help him go farther faster, and his story reveals this important truth: If you want to elevate, you must collaborate.

THE MULTIPLIER EFFECT

I've seen this truth play out repeatedly in business and in life: It's only when someone is willing to enlist the help of others that their story and the reach of their Meaningful Message begin to accelerate and grow.

Some years ago I had the privilege of working with Kaelin Tuell Poulin, the original founder of the LadyBoss Weight Loss brand and author of the book *Big Fat Lies*. Before her LadyBoss journey, Kaelin was a young, overweight woman from a small town in Indiana who went on to become a pro fitness athlete.

Throughout her athletic career, Kaelin learned a lot about how to care for herself and felt her knowledge could help other women reach their own health and fitness goals. She and her husband, Brandon, had started the online LadyBoss community, but they wanted to reach a wider audience for their business by writing a book. They also knew that a book would solidify Kaelin's expertise and raise her brand awareness, spreading her message to people who may never have found her otherwise.

While they knew how to create and run a brand, they needed to collaborate with someone who could capture Kaelin's story in a compelling way. That's where we joined them to create a manuscript that touched the heart with her Meaningful Message and captured her unique process for getting fit.

For those who doubt whether collaboration can truly capture someone's voice in a book, Kaelin is a terrific test case. Two things became clear shortly after the book was released. First, many of her fans and followers said her story brought them to tears as they felt more connected with her than ever. Then Kaelin's book began to accelerate the business growth.

After the book's publication, Kaelin and Brandon expanded the LadyBoss universe with additional health products, a podcast, and more until they were running over $200 million in annual revenue. They eventually sold the company for a significant return. It all began with Kaelin embracing her core message, multiplying the message in a compelling book, and then the two of them building a team to monetize the message and help more people.

Another person I've had the privilege of partnering with is Lewis Howes, host of the popular show *The School of Greatness*. By the time I met Lewis, he had enjoyed considerable success by most standards. After interviewing well over a thousand people who were the best in their fields, Lewis had learned a lot, which had shaped his own voice and experiences as a thought leader on finding healing, fulfillment, and wholeness in life.

In spite of his demanding schedule, Lewis had more books in him, but he needed to make the best use of his time. He knew that if he wanted to maximize his impact and write more books, he would need to elevate through the power of collaboration. Lewis and the StoryBuilders team have since created Howes' multiple *New York Times* bestselling books, including *The Greatness Mindset* and *Make Money Easy.* These and many other IP monetizers we've helped his team create over the years have continued to increase his influence and help drive the continued reach of his message.

If you want to elevate, you must collaborate, which means you must be willing to hold your Meaningful Message loosely.

KNOW YOUR STRENGTHS

What do I mean by "hold your Meaningful Message loosely"? Having a Meaningful Message can cause you to feel conflicted at times. Because your message and your story are unique to you, there can be a tendency to hold them tightly, protecting them to ensure no one steals or misappropriates them.

I understand the concern that someone might borrow your story or message without your permission, but let's just be candid here. The real enemy you face is not piracy but obscurity. People can't steal what they don't know. Sure, you can take steps to legally protect it if appropriate (and putting it in a book is a great start), but the truth is that your message can help you more if you are willing to collaborate with others to tell it well—not to mention the fact that it's just hard work to try to do everything yourself.

No doubt you've experienced the challenge of trying to do it all on your own. You become the limiting factor, the bottleneck through which everything must flow. You become the idea regulator, depriving your message of valuable inputs that could breathe new life into it and take it to new levels.

I know this is true because it happens to me too. Even though I have natural strengths in this area of invention and ideation, I often collaborate with my team or friends and colleagues within my network to benefit from their fresh ideas and insights. I regularly invest in masterminds and engage in forums where I can get new input to enhance my own ideas. It's why I love to work with our StoryPartners to help elevate their ideas—I learn so much in the process as well.

None of us are great at everything. Each of us has unique strengths. When you identify those strengths and structure your work around them, you free everyone to bring their best to any project. So when I say to hold your Meaningful Message loosely, I don't mean to be flexible on what it is; I mean you must be open to collaboration in order to get your message out into the world in the most impactful way possible.

To truly identify and know your strengths, I suggest checking out a couple tools we've used at StoryBuilders to help our team identify and tap into each other's strengths.

First is the RightPath Profile Assessment. This scientifically identifies a person's behavioral hard wiring—what they naturally default to when they're under pressure. We've used it to help everyone on our team find the role that fits their strengths. We are deeply familiar with this specific tool because we've had the privilege of developing resources to support it over the years and have worked with the owner and president, Chris Fuller, on multiple projects. I highly recommend this tool. You can find out more about it at rightpath.com.

Another is the Working Genius Assessment by Patrick Lencioni. It has helped the entire team have an ongoing conversation about what Lencioni identifies as the six components of getting anything done—wonder, invention, discernment, galvanization, enablement, and tenacity. The assessment determines your top two geniuses, your two competencies (you can do them, but you don't necessarily love them), and your two frustrations.

Armed with this self-knowledge, we've been able to help put people in positions they love as well as create cross-departmental teams that work well together. In fact, we even ask each of our StoryPartners to take the Working Genius assessment so we can better understand how they prefer to work. If you want to get things done on any kind of team, explore it further at workinggenius.com.

We need each other to do great things. Creating a collaborative team built on strengths positions you to bring your story and Meaningful Message to life. It accelerates your journey to greater impact, influence, and income.

Who Do You Need?

The challenge of my struggles pales in comparison to the power of our strengths. Together, we can do more.

How will you seize your Story Advantage and tell your story well? How will you multiply your message through a compelling book that transforms lives? How will you monetize your intellectual property to maximize your income in the process? These are questions that must be asked at some point, and you've probably already asked them of yourself while reading this book. Right now, the question you should be asking is not *how will I do it,* but *who can best help me do it?*

> The question you should be asking is not how will I do it, but who can best help me do it?

Who, not *how,* is the question Strategic Coach founder Dan Sullivan and Dr. Benjamin Hardy encourage you to ask if you really want to grow.[4] I have found it to be a key accelerator to maximizing your impact, influence, and income because an expert at everything is an expert at nothing. Don't try to become an expert in everything else that needs to be done to share your story with the world. You simply don't have enough hours in your lifetime to do that. There are certain things you do exceptionally well, and you should continue to focus on doing those things. But someone else has put in the time to become really good at what you need done. So lean into their expertise, and your growth will accelerate exponentially.

That does not mean you can simply "hire and forget." I've made that mistake before. I thought I found an expert who knew more than I did, so I simply let them take charge of my dream. I didn't fully engage. I didn't hold them accountable for results. I didn't just take my hands off the wheel, I got out of the car entirely while it was still moving forward without me. The results weren't good.

No one cares about your Meaningful Message like you do, so you need to stay engaged and own the outcome. But rely on the expertise of others to inform your decision-making as you continue to hold the steering wheel of your dreams loosely.

YOUR MESSAGE PARTNER CHECKLIST

Now that you know your strengths and understand you can't do everything alone, who do you need to help develop your Story EcoSystem™?

First, keep in mind that this is a process. I've heard this saying expressed in many ways and ascribed to different people, but the one that has stuck with me goes like this. People overestimate how much they can do in one year and underestimate how much they can do in three years. In other words, if you try to rush too quickly, you'll end up doing much less than you think. But if you invest the time to intentionally build your story well, you'll reap sustainable benefits.

Building your story in a way that maximizes your impact, influence, and income takes intentional action made consistently over time. There's something to be said for the magical power of persistence on your story-development journey. The key is finding the balance between doggedly moving forward and not getting so far out in front of yourself that you block your own progress.

You want to find message partners—people who are both willing to question why you're doing what you're doing and elevate your ideas to the next level. Start with these people.

- **Idea People:** I suspect you have some ideas of your own or you wouldn't be reading this book. But whatever ideas you have can always be elevated with synergy from the ideas of others. Idea people can generate something out of nothing or add value to what you already have in ways you never imagined. Be warned: When you invite idea people into your world, be prepared to have your status quo disrupted. Know that you don't have to act on all or even any of the ideas. You can put some ideas into action on the field. You can store other ideas in the locker room for now. Or you can cut them entirely from your team if they don't fit your dream. The choice is yours.

- **Strategy People:** These people can help you make choices. Once you've generated the ideas, you need people to help you discern which ideas you should pursue, when you should pursue them, and how you should best take action. Think of these people as idea filters. If an idea gets past them, there's a good chance it has merit. These are not the same as the idea people, and they are not the execution people, but they are critical at honing ideas to help you take your message to the next level.

- **Action People:** For many years, I did not realize the importance of having action people, or "galvanizers" as Lencioni describes them in *The 6 Types of Working Genius*. I simply wasn't one of them, and I knew that because I coached high school girls basketball for one season back in the day. Even though we somehow had a winning record for the year, I discovered that I was not wired to be a basketball coach because I truly didn't have any desire to galvanize the team to take action. I saw the strategy and had the ideas for helping the team succeed, but getting them fired up to give 110 percent on the court? Not for me.

Because I do not have that natural strength, I've come to appreciate the value of people who have a built-in action bias. They are able to leverage their unique wiring to motivate people to take action in a way that I simply cannot. Once again, that's okay, but knowing this is an area of frustration for me enables me to partner with others for whom it is a strength. As a team, we can then get a lot more of my ideas done.

- **Execution People:** Speaking of getting things done, every project depends on people who can actually do that. These critical people enjoy getting their hands dirty, metaphorically or literally. They thrive on taking a project across the finish line themselves or helping others do so. I have a little bit of this wiring within me personally, but others on our team simply excel at it, and I am in awe of their abilities.

  A word of caution: If you are naturally wired to get things done, you may tend to undervalue the idea people and the strategy people. You'll need to intentionally not jump from having an idea to acting on it before you've generated a list of great ideas and decided which ones would be best to pursue.

- **Administrative People:** You need people to keep track of everything. You just do. That may be finances, followers, records, statistics, analytics—all of them and then some. Certain people love doing this and are naturally wired to excel at it. When you find them, hold onto them. Give them clear direction, set up healthy accountability, and then let them do their thing. When administrative people deliver their best to you, they become almost invisible even as they become more invaluable. (Hint: Make sure to let them know how much you appreciate them. You'll thank me for this later.)

- **Influence People:** To help get the word out about your message, you need relationships with people outside your core team who have connections to your audience or customers. These people have already built followings and forums where the people who would most benefit from your message already hang out. By connecting with and adding value to these influencers, you create the potential for partnerships that would expose their audience to your message. I could write a whole book about this. Instead, I'll recommend "Habit Four: The Mastermind Habit" from the book *Make Money Easy* by Lewis Howes. It contains terrific advice on how to go about developing critical connections with influencers.

- **Accountability People:** These people can be easy to overlook until it's too late. That's why I suggest you find them early on your journey and keep engaging with them. As you grow, you need people in your life to hold you accountable and keep you from "message drift." These are people who are willing to ask the tough questions about your vision, your work, and your life. They are people with whom you can be brutally honest, knowing they want the best for you and are willing to speak the truth to you as well. Having these people in your life can keep you from drifting away from the mission that once moved you to make the world a better place.

This checklist serves as a terrific start to help you identify the people to whom you need to tell your story well and maximize your influence, impact, and income—and go farther, faster.

GET ALIGNED, THEN GET STARTED

There is one critical thing you should look for in anyone you collaborate with. Our team at StoryBuilders may be a good fit to partner with you to do a lot of the things I've shared in this book; however, we may not be that good fit, and that's okay. Here's why. One of the most important elements for any partnership to work is alignment, which includes message alignment. You want to work with people who resonate with and support your message. You don't want people who simply crank out word widgets without really supporting the heart of what you're sharing.

> You want to work with people who resonate with and support your message.

If your message is promoting a controversial topic, for example, you should not look for the most talented people to collaborate with you. You should look for the most talented people *who share your perspective* on that topic to collaborate with you because talent alone is not enough. You need to connect at a deeper, heart-and-soul level. That's part of what alignment means.

Another important element of alignment is simply making sure you share the same values. Our core values at

StoryBuilders guide everything we do. As Greg Cagle has taught us over the years, values serve as our decision-making filters. If you and your storytelling partners value different things, then you will naturally make different decisions.

Our core values at StoryBuilders drive us to CREATE a story worth telling:

C   **Creativity:** We always ask "what if" before figuring out "how to."

R   **Relationships:** We always put people before profit.

E   **Excellence:** We either do it exceptionally well or not at all.

A   **Authenticity:** We always stay true to who we are and do what we say we will do.

T   **Teamwork:** Our struggles are always solved by our strengths.

E   **Energy**: We always prioritize healthy, holistic living to achieve sustainable success for our team and our families.

Following Greg's advice in the book *The 4 Dimensions of Culture*, we added a hill-to-die-on statement: *If we do nothing else, we will … Make It Matter.* Whatever situation we may face, we want to do what will have the greatest positive impact for our StoryPartners, our team, and the world. Your values may be different than ours, and that's okay, but you want to always choose partners whose values naturally align closely with yours.

The final alignment element you want to seek with your storytelling partners is what I call chemistry. To put it bluntly, you actually want to like the people you work with and enjoy spending time with them. It takes time and energy to create a compelling BrandStory, write a great book, or design a learning experience. It's important that it feels like time well spent.

I encourage you to take what you've learned in this book to find your storytelling partners who help you tell your story well and share it with the world. Whatever you do, don't try to do it alone. Every story matters, and the world deserves to hear what you have to say.

THE COLLABORATIVE BOOK EXPERIENCE

It's been said that 80 percent of people say they want to write a book at some point in their lives. I actually think it's higher than that. I've rarely been in a room where every hand didn't go up when I asked if anyone had thought about writing a book. A lot of us have that idea, but only 1 percent of us ever do. Many people dream of becoming an author, but very few people actually follow through on that dream.

I shared more about all the benefits of writing a book in Chapter 4, so I won't revisit all of them here. However, of the 1 percent who actually do write a book, more than 77 percent try to do it themselves. Don't get me wrong. I'm not trivializing the people who try to do it themselves—not at all. I applaud them for pursuing their dream. But there's a major downside to trying to create a great book by yourself.

I'm sure you've seen some of those DIY or self-published books that were obviously written and designed with, shall we say, less than professional support. Most people can spot the difference between a professionally published book and a purely self-published book. They might be polite and not say anything about it, but they notice.

That quality difference can create a lot of friction for your message. That is why at StoryBuilders, we partner with entrepreneurs, business professionals, and thought leaders to create books that are not only highly creative but also exude excellence in every way.

That's the power of collaboration. Those who choose to do it themselves must live with the reality that they can only take it so far and make it so good since no one can be an expert at everything. Those who choose to collaborate release the power of others, the ones who are experts in writing and publishing, to make the book better than it ever could have been as a solo project.

The worst part, though, is how many ideas end up in the book graveyard having never been written and thus never read. More than that, it's a loss of positive impact and lives changed for the better as well.

I get it. Life happens. I have a book of my own that I began writing twenty-five years ago. It's a fiction book based loosely on a story found in the Bible. I love the idea of taking stories that are fairly well-known by certain audiences and building out what might have been going on behind the scenes and in the cracks between the facts. So why is this book still unfinished? To tell the truth, it got stuck. I got about two-thirds of the way through drafting it, and then other life priorities pushed it out of the way.

Even though I've written all sorts of bestselling books, I still haven't made it back to finish that one. Now that I'm actually mentioning it here, I have a little healthy accountability to force myself to finish it. But I always tried to do it on my own and thus haven't gotten it done—yet. (If you run into me somewhere, can you help me out and ask how my fiction book is coming?)

There are any number of other reasons that might be holding you back from bringing your book to life. The first one is simply ignorance—you just don't know how to do it. Sure, maybe you have ideas in your head, but what's the best way to get them out of your head and into a format that could become a book? How do you organize it, trim it, and make sure it is focused for the reader? Then how do you make sure it flows well for a great reader experience? And once you do get something onto paper, how do you get it edited? (You will want someone to edit it if you want it to be good.) How do you figure out the best publishing path to bring it to life? Then how do you share it with the rest of the world?

All the steps involved in the process can feel overwhelming. But it doesn't have to be if you work with a team that can help you navigate the process. In the moment of decision, that sense of overwhelm can cause us to simply push it aside for the time being, and next thing you know, twenty-five years have passed and you still haven't written it. Or worse, you've run out of time all together.

The truth is you'll never know the possible impact your book could have if you don't write it.

The second thing holding people back is a lack of confidence. Especially when you talk about putting ideas or Meaningful Message out into the world, there can be a nagging suspicion that no one will want to read it. What if you do all that work and no one shows up?

It doesn't matter who you are or how much you've accomplished in your life, we're all plagued by self-doubt to some extent. The reality is that with any book, there must be a strategy to support getting the word out. StoryBuilders can help with that, too, but the first step is to write a really great book.

You may be right. Perhaps no one will want to read the book you want to write. But that doesn't mean you don't have an idea worth writing about. You may simply need to collaborate with others who can help you focus and elevate your message and tell it in a way that resonates with the audience you want to reach. The truth is you'll never know the possible impact your book could have if you don't write it. When you reach the end of your time on this earth, would you rather be saying, "I wish I would've written that book" or experience the peace that comes from knowing you made the world a better place by releasing a message that will touch lives long after you're gone?

A third excuse I often hear for not bringing your book to life is that you're not a writer. To that I say, *What difference does that make?*

I suppose I should explain a little bit. Remember that if you want to *elevate*, you must *collaborate*. If you are thinking about writing a book on your own, you may be wondering how on earth someone could collaborate to write a book.

Here's a little secret: More books than you realize are not written by the authors themselves. That's not to say those books don't contain the authors' ideas or messages. It just means someone else came alongside that author—someone whose strength is writing and storytelling—to help bring the book to life. A lot of the books with well-known names on the covers weren't written by those authors themselves for a number of reasons.

Perhaps the author is a speaker, not a writer. This is certainly true with John C. Maxwell. He has been a popular public speaker and thought leader for decades, and he also has been open about his writing partnership with Charlie Wetzel. One of John's many strengths is that he knew he was a gifted speaker and thinker but not a gifted writer. So early in his career, he partnered with someone who *was* a gifted writer to help bring his ideas into book form in his voice. It has been a winning partnership that has fueled John's ability to produce more than a hundred books to date, impacting millions of lives. John does what he does best. Charlie does what he does best. Between them, they're able to tell John's message in a way that makes the world a much better place.

If you check the acknowledgments in the back of a lot of books, you'll often find references to key folks who helped bring them to life. I have never seen a popular book without a page thanking the team that helped, and I've certainly never seen one that simply said, "I did all this myself." That's not how it works. In other words, you don't have to (and really shouldn't try to) do it all yourself. The most successful people I know can find a better use of their time than trying to master the art of writing, storytelling, and navigating the ins and outs of publishing. It's better to partner with a team that can guide you through the journey with a proven process so you can keep doing what you're already successfully doing.

And if you're worried that the book won't sound like you, don't be. The right team will make sure it sounds exactly like you. We work with people all the time to craft books that fit their unique voice. Our aim is to write a book that will make the people closest to them say, "That sounds just like you."

But if you would still rather do the writing yourself, that's fine too. You can always enlist a coaching team like ours to help lay the foundation for your book and provide healthy accountability and guidance as you do the work.

Your story advantage can be turned into an incredible tool for great good in the world if you are willing to elevate your message through collaboration. But the truth is, none of the help matters if you don't believe you have a story worth telling.

YOUR ADVANTAGE ACTIVITIES

If you own or run a business, you know it takes a village to keep everything rolling smoothly (unless you're a business of one doing something very specific, but even then, you probably have at least an accountant or bookkeeper). So why would you try to build your Story EcoSystem™ on your own when you don't need to?

> Your story advantage can be turned into an incredible tool for great good in the world if you are willing to elevate your message through collaboration.

Even if you start the process alone, at some point you will need help to finish it. We all do. That's where the following assessment will help you identify what kind of person or team you need right now to start spreading your Meaningful Message in a way that maximizes your influence, impact, and income.

THE MESSAGE PARTNER ASSESSMENT

For each statement below, select the choice that best describes you to help identify who you need to help you keep moving forward.

1. I have lots of ideas but struggle to choose or narrow them down.

   A. I always get stuck in idea overwhelm.
   B. I sometimes need help filtering what's worth pursuing.
   C. I usually know which idea to go with.
   D. I don't struggle with this—I'm naturally decisive.

   → *[If A/B: You may need an **Idea Person**.]*

2. I take action, but often without a clear plan.

   A. I jump into things without thinking them through.
   B. I sometimes act too fast and regret it later.
   C. I prefer a clear plan but will act when needed.
   D. I always take time to plan before taking action.

   → *[If A/B: You may need a **Strategy Person**.]*

3. I have a clear plan but rarely follow through or complete things.

   A. I rarely finish projects I start.
   B. I lose momentum partway through.

C. I usually finish things, but not always on time.

D. I'm highly consistent with execution.

→ *[If A/B: You may need an **Execution Person** or **Action Person**.]*

4. I avoid marketing or promoting myself or my work.

    A. I never talk about what I do publicly.

    B. I promote occasionally but feel awkward doing it.

    C. I promote when I have to, but not by choice.

    D. I'm comfortable sharing my work with the world.

    → *[If A/B: You may need an **Influence Person**.]*

5. I feel disorganized and lose track of important steps or tools.

    A. I constantly misplace files, links, and plans.

    B. I'm semi-organized, but it takes a lot of effort.

    C. I manage okay with reminders and systems.

    D. I'm naturally organized and on top of details.

    → *[If A/B: You may need an **Administrative Person**.]*

6. I don't have anyone to hold me accountable or check in.

    A. I work in isolation and often feel stuck.

    B. I sometimes wish I had someone to check in with.

    C. I have some support, but it's inconsistent.

    D. I have strong accountability in place already.

    → *[If A/B: You may need an **Accountability Person**.]*

My hope is that you're excited to get your Meaningful Message out into the world right this very second. But if you're still on the fence, I understand. You may just need to know a little secret that changes everything.

If you want more support to act on what you learn in this book, visit *YourStoryAdvantage.com/FreeResources* or scan the QR code to discover FREE resources to help you maximize your story.

8

The Secret Ingredient

Why do we love stories so much? When we were young, we all asked our parents or grandparents to tell us stories. Now what do we do when we have free time? We binge stories on Netflix or read more books. It's as if we just can't get enough stories.

I think we love them because we long to experience one of our own, to go on an expedition that requires the courage to dream for a cause we believe in, even in the face of great risk. We want our lives to become dramatic tales of adventure in which we take on impossible challenges and find deep meaning and even deeper

This day is a paragraph that is being written right now in your story, but will it be a story worth telling?

fulfillment instead of only pretending that our story actually meant something.

The reality is that each of us is living a story right now. This moment is a word or phrase on one of the pages of your life. This day is a paragraph that is being written right now in your story, but will it be a story worth telling?

I suppose we could take the approach of Mark Twain, the famous author known for his rather cynical views on life. Here's what he thought about the value of our stories.

> We are blown upon the world, we float buoyantly upon the summer air a little while, complacently showing off our grace of form and our dainty iridescent colors, then we vanish with a little puff, leaving behind nothing but a memory—and sometimes not even that. I suppose at those times when we wake in the depth of the night and reflect, there is not one of us who is not willing to confess to only being a soap bubble, and as little worth the making.

Only a soap bubble—of little worth. Yikes, Mark. I'm no party planner, but I wouldn't suggest inviting him to host your next bash unless you want everyone to leave feeling pretty depressed.

When I think of what the soap-bubble life might look like, I think of living a story that may be busy on the outside but feel empty on the inside. It's a life defined by drifting aimlessly without any meaningful purpose, one where you complain about what happens to you and see yourself as a victim of circumstances beyond your control. The soap-bubble life is all about avoiding discomfort as you sit back and coast. The problem with that approach is that coasting only goes in one direction—downhill.

On our better days, however, I don't think any of us really agree with Twain's cynicism, do we? We sense deep within that our story should be more than a colorful bubble destined to pop without leaving a trace. We lean more naturally toward the poet Walt Whitman who expressed the innate human desire "that the powerful play goes on, and you may contribute a verse" to humanity's song. We want to make the world a better place than when we arrived. We want to do something that truly makes a difference and leaves a legacy long after we're gone.

I told you in Chapter 1 about my own journey to step away from my safe, secure job to pursue a deeper calling. That experience taught me a lot about something that is vital for those who want to fully maximize their story advantage and contribute a meaningful verse. Think of it as the secret ingredient that fuels, guides, and sustains you on this journey to live a story you can share with the world to maximize your impact, influence, and income.

What is that secret ingredient? Faith.

THE SECRET IS IN THE DOING

I don't necessarily mean faith in a religious sense, although that certainly fuels and guides my own journey to serve others. I'm talking more about the faith you must have to truly live a story worth telling, to tap into your unique story advantage and build a thriving Story EcoSystem™.

Living a story worth telling requires you to step into the unknown, a place where you aren't sure what will happen next. It calls you to confront your deepest fears, biggest personal giants, and darkest villains. The journey demands that you endure the discomfort of change and the potential for deep disappointment. In short, living a story worth telling is not easy. That's why most people settle for a story that is anything but worth telling. They choose safety over significance, comfort over lasting legacy, and soap bubbles instead of a Meaningful Message.

Doing something meaningful and lasting with your story will require faith. The good news is that when it comes down to it, faith isn't all that complicated. Here is how I define it:

Doing what you believe to be true often in spite of what you see, sense, or feel.

Note the three main parts:

1. **Doing.** Our stories will be written by what we do. That seems obvious enough. A little less obvious is that what we do is determined by what we believe to be true. For example, if you don't believe your story can

help others, you'll never take action to help anyone. You may say you want to, but until you act on what you say you believe, you don't really know what you believe. You only discover what you truly believe when your actions bring challenging consequences. Only then do you discover what you believe. Your motion reveals your devotion to what you believe to be true. In short, faith isn't faith until it's tested.

2. **What you believe to be true.** Think back on the stories you love. Aren't they stories of heroes who took on the impossible because of something they believed in, whether a cause, person, country, or dream? Think of the Avengers who save the universe against impossible odds time and again. Or think of the heroes who sacrifice to stand up to the invaders on Pandora in the *Avatar* movies. Few stories resonate with us like those whose characters laid it all on the line for what they believed. Even visionaries like Walt Disney, humanitarians like Mother Teresa, and ambitious businessmen such as Steve Jobs were motivated by what they believed to be true about life and their own unique roles in the world.

3. **Often in spite of what you see, sense, or feel.** Living with faith does not mean that what you believe must always contradict what you see. Too often we make the assumption that we must choose between seeing and believing, as if you can't have one if you have the

other. In fact, if what we believe is true, then what we experience should line up with what we believe most of the time. But our limited senses can take us only so far, and they can be quite misleading. Some days the script playing in your head will tell you that you'll never make it. Another day your inner voice will whisper you're not worthy or your message isn't good enough to help anyone.

What if instead of a Soap-Bubble Life you chose to live a Faith-Focused Life, one driven by faith and not by fear? The Faith-Focused Life sees circumstances as happening *for* you and not *to* you. It embraces the adventure ahead and sets out to create meaningful moments that make the world a better place. It is a life committed to stewarding your story well, living intentionally, and being willing to share your struggles as well as your successes so others may learn from them. Remember, your story is about you, but ultimately it isn't for you.

WHAT WILL YOU DO WITH YOUR STORY?

I encourage you to ask yourself this clarifying question: Could someone identify your dreams by examining your life? Based on your day-to-day actions, what do you believe to be true about your own Meaningful Message? How seriously do you see yourself as a steward of your one story? Do you believe your story gives you a unique advantage, an opportunity to make a difference in the world in a way that maximizes your impact, influence, and income?

If you answered *yes*, even a hesitant *yes*, then you have to ask this question: What will you do next with your story? Will you revisit the earlier chapters in this book and work through the exercises? Will you visit the StoryBuilder site to get more resources to help you get clarity on your Meaningful Message? Will you choose to bring your book to life as your Message Multiplier? Will you begin building your unique IP in a way that positions you to monetize your message and reach more people to make the world a better place?

Whatever that best next move might be for you, it all starts with deciding right here and right now to do whatever it takes to steward your story well. Your breakthrough begins when you start with your story and decide to become a StoryBuilder. You join the movement of people committed to making the world a better place by harnessing the power of their unique stories.

When you do, you find the:

- **Faith** to believe your story matters and act on your belief.

- **Courage** to share your pain in a way that helps other people heal.

- **Resolve** to persist through the messiness to shift perspectives and bring about transformation.

- **Passion** to persist through the challenges that threaten to derail you.

- **Words** that touch someone else's heart and mind.

- **Freedom** from fears that say you're not enough.

- **Advantage** you need to maximize your impact, influence, and income.

Don't waste your story. The StoryBuilder cheerfully answers the call to serve others through your story, willing to push through the discomfort of growth to help "contribute a verse" to humanity's song. Will that be you? The choice is yours. Don't waste your story.

EVERY STORY MATTERS

One final note: Let me be clear about something. You may not be someone who wants to build your Story EcoSystem™. You may not have any desire to write a book. You may not want to build a business, increase your influence, or make more money by serving other people through your story. And that's okay.

You can still be a StoryBuilder.

Your story still matters. How do I know? Simple. Every story matters.

Just like Horton in the classic Dr. Seuss tale, a story is a story no matter how small it may seem to be. The truth is there are no small stories. Each one is significant—especially yours. Who you are matters. What you do matters. You have a story advantage just like everyone else. Each of us does. The only question is this: What will you do with it?

I believe each of us has a unique calling to fulfill, something no one else can do in the way we do it. Only you can know with certainty what that calling is. Only you know what deeply resonates within your soul.

When I was leading a school, I was doing good work. I was helping students and families in a very real way. In fact, I still hear from students many years later about the positive impact I had on them. Everyone told me at the time how much they appreciated what I was doing, but only I knew I had a deeper calling to fulfill. Only I sensed the unrealized potential within me. And only I could do something about it.

Maybe that's you. Maybe you've sensed that you have a message burning within you that you want to—no, *need* to—share with the world. Perhaps you've kept it tucked away inside until now. Perhaps you've tried to get it out and even had some success doing it.

You may even have had quite a bit of success sharing your Meaningful Message with the world, but you still think there could be or even *should* be more impact. I get it. I've worked with a lot of people over the years just like you, so I understand the excitement, frustration, tension, and everything else that goes with it.

That's why I chose to become a StoryBuilder—to help people just like you tell their stories well and make the world a better place. I founded an organization of like-minded people committed to coming alongside you to elevate your message to maximize your impact, influence, and income.

For more than ten years, we've worked with hundreds of StoryPartners, from well-known names to names you may not have heard of yet. We've written numerous *New York Times* and *USA Today* bestsellers and created dynamic IP that makes money for our StoryPartners every day.

But the most satisfying part of what we do happens when we hear stories of the impact on people from the messages we've helped shape. That's what it's all about for us—making the world a better place by helping people like you maximize your story advantage.

We look forward to hearing what you do with your story.

If you want more support to act on what you
learn in this book, visit *YourStoryAdvantage.com/
FreeResources* or scan the QR code to discover
FREE resources to help you maximize your story.

YOUR Story
ADVANTAGE Academy

STOP READING.
START DOING!

The people who actually transform their message into greater impact, influence, and income aren't just readers—they're doers.

Your Story Advantage Academy is the complete implementation system designed to transform your message into tangible impact, influence, and income.

This isn't just theory. It's a proven path that has helped hundreds of thought leaders, entrepreneurs, and business professionals:

- **Gain CLARITY** that cuts through the noise.

- **Build instant CREDIBILITY** as the go-to expert.

- **Create multiple INCOME STREAMS** from your core message.

- **Reach MORE PEOPLE** with less effort.

- **STAND OUT** in a crowded marketplace.

- **Build MOMENTUM** as your ecosystem thrives.

Each module includes impactful video lessons with Bill Blankschaen, fillable PDF workbooks, and clear action steps—plus access to a community of StoryBuilders to encourage you along the way.

Imagine…

- A complete and compelling BrandStory in weeks.

- A clear framework for *your* expert, brand-defining book.

- A unique roadmap for income-generating IP assets.

Secure your seat in Your Story Advantage Academy!

Visit *YourStoryAdvantageAcademy.com* today!

ACKNOWLEDGMENTS

Every story intertwines with so many others to become the richest version of itself. And so it is with each of us and this book in particular.

Special thanks to my wife Faith, whose love and support for the storytelling dream fueled this journey. This book could not have been created without her.

Thank you to the entire talented StoryBuilders team, without whom this book would simply not be possible. You took good ideas and made them infinitely better. Your passion for storytelling and care for our StoryPartners sets you apart. It is a privilege to lead and create alongside each of you.

Thank you to all the StoryPartners we have served thus far. You have given us the opportunity to come alongside and serve and learn so we could be positioned to serve even more people. Your trust and support made this book and the ideas in it come to life in very real ways.

And to all the storytelling giants, too numerous to name, on whose shoulders I stand, thank you for your tireless work to inspire others to live and share a story worth telling.

Finally, thank you to the ultimate StoryTeller who makes every story matter and invites each of us to be part of His greater, grace-filled story.

ABOUT THE AUTHOR

Bill Blankschaen is the founder and Chief Story Architect of StoryBuilders, a creative team of story-tellers who share his passion for helping people live a story worth telling and serving them with excellence in genuine, high-trust relationships. StoryBuilders tells stories that make the world a better place by creating compelling books and learning experiences that turn ideas into greater impact, influence, and income.

A multiple *New York Times* and *USA Today* Best Selling writer, Bill and his team work with a variety of influencers like John C. Maxwell and Maxwell Leadership, Lewis Howes, Dean Graziosi, Kevin Harrington from *Shark Tank*, Michael Hyatt (Full Focus), Zig Ziglar and family, Jeff Allen, Jason Wilson, entrepreneurs, corporate leaders, business coaches and consultants, political figures, cultural voices, athletes, comedians, fitness gurus, psychologists, and even faith leaders at some of the largest churches in America. The books, resources, and experiences they have created have already impacted millions of people—and they're just getting started.

ENDNOTES

1 Seth Godin, "Reject the Tyranny of Being Picked: Pick Yourself," Seth's Blog, March 21, 2011, https://seths.blog/2011/03/reject-th e-tyranny-of-being-picked-pick-yourself/.

2 Kate Taylor, "How Chick-fil-A Got Its Name," Business Insider, Sept. 4, 2019.

3 Rory Vaden and AJ Vaden, Wealthy and Well-Known: Build Your Personal Brand and Turn Your Reputation into Revenue (Mission Driven Press, 2025).

4 Dan Sullivan and Dr. Benjamin Hardy, Who Not How: The Formula to Achieve Bigger Goals Through Accelerating Teamwork (Hay House Business, 2020).

www.ingramcontent.com/pod-product-compliance
Lightning Source LLC
Chambersburg PA
CBHW071213210326
41597CB00016B/1795